Penguin

Weird W

Charlotte Harper is a journalist at the *Sydney Morning Herald*, where she scours the Internet for her Saturday column, 'Charlotte's Web', in the Icon section (www.smh.com.au/icon/). She also writes regularly for the *Herald*'s sport section, produces content for Fairfax's web sites, and can be heard on ABC NewsRadio on Sunday evenings chatting about the Web.

At 27 years old, Charlotte lives halfway between her favourite beach and bookshop in Sydney.

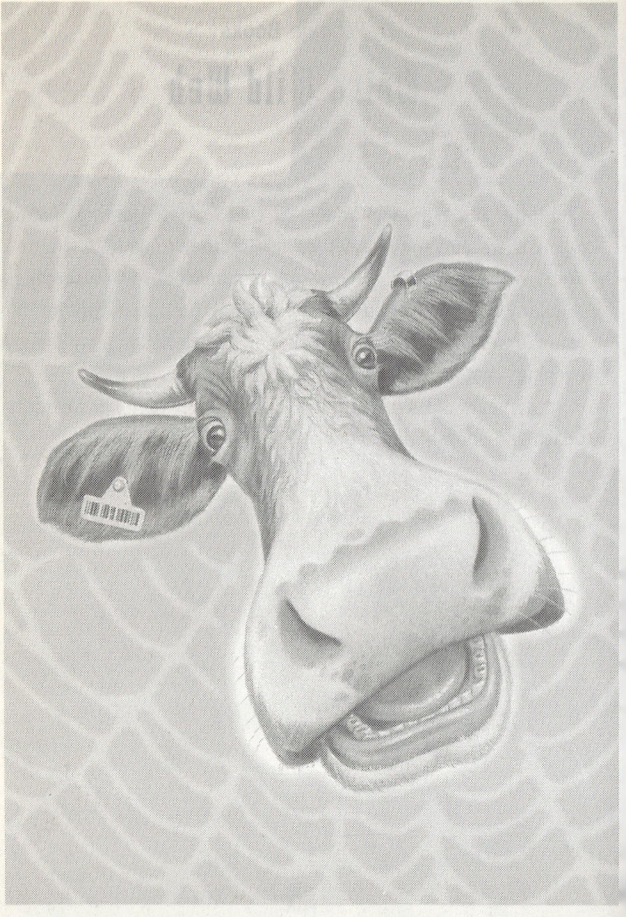

Weird wild web

Charlotte Harper

Penguin Books

Penguin Books Australia Ltd
487 Maroondah Highway, PO Box 257
Ringwood, Victoria 3134, Australia
Penguin Books Ltd
Harmondsworth, Middlesex, England
Penguin Putnam Inc.
375 Hudson Street, New York, New York 10014, USA
Penguin Books Canada Limited
10 Alcorn Avenue, Toronto, Ontario, Canada M4V 3B2
Penguin Books (NZ) Ltd
Cnr Rosedale and Airborne Roads, Albany, Auckland, New Zealand
Penguin Books (South Africa) (Pty) Ltd
5 Watkins Street, Denver Ext 4, 2094, South Africa
Penguin Books India (P) Ltd
11, Community Centre, Panchsheel Park, New Delhi 110 017, India

First published by Penguin Books Australia Ltd 1999

1 3 5 7 9 10 8 6 4 2

Copyright © Charlotte Harper 1999

All rights reserved. Without limiting the rights under copyright reserved above, no part of this publication may be reproduced, stored in or introduced into a retrieval system, or transmitted, in any form or by any means (electronic, mechanical, photocopying, recording or otherwise), without the prior written permission of both the copyright owner and the above publisher of this book.

Designed by Melissa Fraser, Penguin Design Studio
Typeset in Meta 8.5/12pt by Midland Typesetters, Maryborough, Victoria
Printed in Australia by Australian Print Group, Maryborough, Victoria

National Library of Australia
Cataloguing-in-Publication data:

Harper, Charlotte, 1971– .
Weird wild web.
ISBN 0 14 028278 5.
1. Web sites – Directories. I. Title.
025.04

www.penguin.com.au

Contents

Publisher's note	vi
Introduction	1
1 Games and Other Time Wasters	4
2 Media	22
3 Sporty Stuff	34
4 Music	55
5 Fans and Anti-fans	65
6 Up Close and Personal	76
7 Shopping	89
8 Being There	104
9 Good Causes	119
10 Kids and School	130
11 DIY	147
12 Awards	157
13 Truly Weird	165
14 Geek City	181
15 Bare Essentials	193
Acknowledgements	210
Credits	211
Index	214

Publisher's note

It has not always been possible for us to trace the original sources for the illustrative material used in this book, as these sources were located on the World Wide Web. However, our known sources are detailed in the acknowledgements on page 210.

The content of the web sites listed in this book, due to the constantly changing face of the World Wide Web, may change considerably from the content cited at the time of publication. Penguin Books therefore cannot be held responsible for the content, or the accessibility, of those sites listed.

Introduction

Welcome to the weird wild Web.

I'm a media junkie from way back. But during the 1980s, I became dissatisfied. No existing medium, library, newsagent, music or bookshop gave me all the news, information and gossip I wanted, when I wanted it. Then in the early 1990s, along came my salvation: the Web.

It's better than a newsagent filled with newspapers and magazines because its content is (mostly) free, accessible from wherever you are on earth, and archived. It's better than a library because it's always new (we like new) and no one's torn out the page you want to read. It's better than a bookshop because the content is cheap, easy on shelf space, but still beautifully packaged (online bookshops will also save you the trip and they tend to sell books cheaply). Oh, and the Web's not just words and pictures either; there are audio, video, dialogue and forums, too.

It's better than television because you can find out the cricket scores now, not after the ad break (or not at all because *A Current Affair*'s more important). You can jump to a site to read a biography of someone featured in a story rather than hope that Mike Munro will ask him or her that one question you're dying to know the answer to. And it brings you Triple J wherever you are in the world.

Weird Wild Web is a snapshot taken through the eyes of someone who spends a lot of time surfing the Web, who talks to the like-minded or totally off-the-wall types about what works and what doesn't. It's a taste of what has been seen, heard and interacted with online, and will give you a series of starting points to help navigate the often overwhelming mass of information out there. (If you're an inexperienced Net user, you might like to start with the Bare Essentials chapter.)

The book is not intended to be a comprehensive guide to what's available on the Internet. That would be an impossible task because of the diversity and vast number of sites that exist, and because there are new and worthy sites popping up every hour, just as fascinating and fun sites close down or change addresses. So forgive me if you find the odd site listed in the following pages has moved or disappeared since the book's printing. I've done everything I can to ensure that the book is up to date, but the virtual realms are as ever-changing as the lives of the individuals, organisations and communities they come from.

You can use the book in a number of ways, because people use the Web in different ways and for a variety of reasons. If you're new to all this, dip in to get a feel for what's available. Visit a few sites, then follow their links to other places that fulfil your needs and desires. You might prefer to read up on and select staple news, sport and entertainment sites, then stick with them.

If you're as familiar with the Web as your TV set, then use this book to remind you to take up exploring again. Plenty of sensational stuff has appeared out there since you last settled on your favourites and bookmarked them.

Most of the sites found their way here because someone emailed me the address with a note raving about it, because I stumbled across it while using a search engine (here at the *Weird Wild Web*, we recommend www.dogpile.com for searching) to find something far less interesting, or because I just wondered whether there would be a site on a particular person/topic/activity, and happily found that there was.

The sites get a mark out of five for content, speed, looks and structure. There's no point in posting and promoting brilliant online content if your site takes twenty minutes to load into a browser. Similarly, if it looks ugly and is riddled with typos and spelling errors, users will click their way elsewhere before they realise it's worth exploring. If it's too hard to navigate, a fair whack of your content and effort is wasted. You don't have to be a rocket scientist to work these things out, but you'd be surprised at how many major sites fail on at least one count at some time or another. Still, the ratings are only a guide, and totally subjective, as are the reviews.

Don't take my word for it: get online and visit them yourself. Once you've done that, collect 200 or so book-worthy (or at least bookmark-worthy) sites of your own, and send the best to me for the next edition!

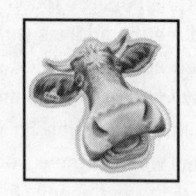

one

Games and Other Time Wasters

Remember playing Solitaire on the computer when you should have been studying or working? If the answer's yes, then your boss/lecturer/parents will want to hide this section from you. Imagine how much more time you can waste when there are hundreds of games to choose from! The following sites are just the beginning. Many of them appear on mega-games sites that provide hours of distraction in their own right. Some of them require plug-ins (see page 197), but they'll let you know if you need to download one, and tell you where to go to get it. Once you have the plug-ins, you can play just about anything on the Web. Enjoy.

Rack 'em up
http://shockrave.macromedia.com/content/skyworks/pool/

Sydney Morning Herald Internet staff have nobly sacrificed days of their lives to test the validity of online pool games in order to report that this version, on Macromedia's ShockRave site, is it. It's the only one that lets you play against another person or against the game itself, and you get to choose the exact angle and strength of each shot. Try it and say goodbye to tolerating Cat Stevens on the jukebox in pool halls.

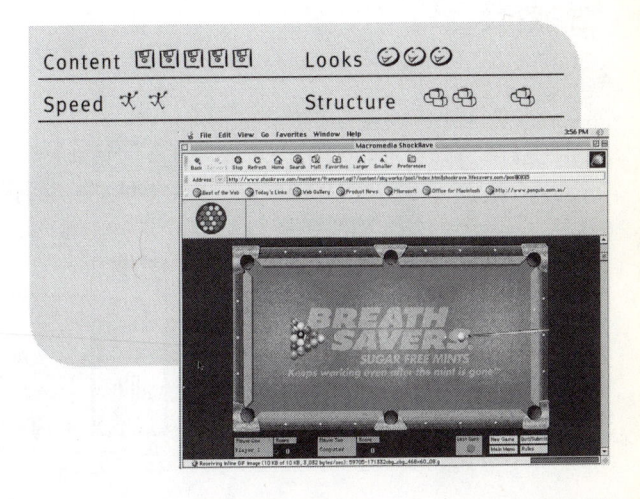

Content	🎞🎞🎞🎞🎞	Looks	☺☺☺
Speed	☆☆	Structure	♣♣ ♣

Finger twister

http://www.spin.co.uk/shock/twist/twist.html

Use your mouse to spin the Twister colour and digit selector, then get your fingers and a friend's entangled all over your no-longer-pristine, print-free PC screen. This virtual Twister game will send clean-screen colleagues and family members into a spin.

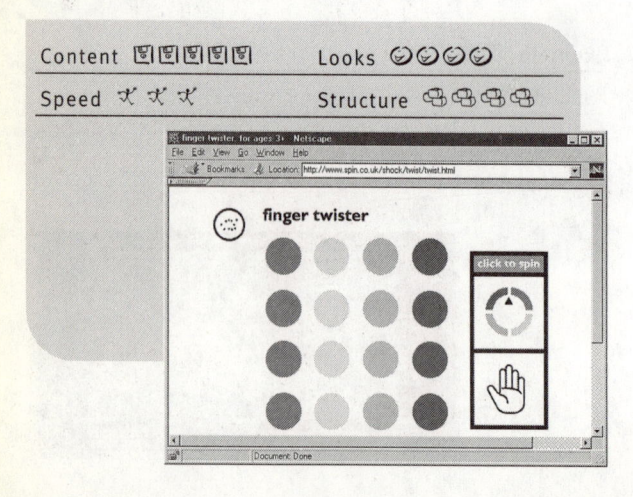

Content 🖻🖻🖻🖻🖻   Looks ☺☺☺☺

Speed ✼ ✼ ✼   Structure ✿✿✿✿

Pacman lives
http://www.netconnect.com.au/laughsonline/games/pac/

For some reason, back in the days of video-game arcades, Pacman seemed less violent than Space Invaders. After all, eating a flashing ghost is nothing compared with blasting an entire galaxy's space fleet to bits. This Shockwave version of the munching maze game is cheaper than the 1970s or 1980s milk-bar equivalent, but it's not quite as much fun without the sound.

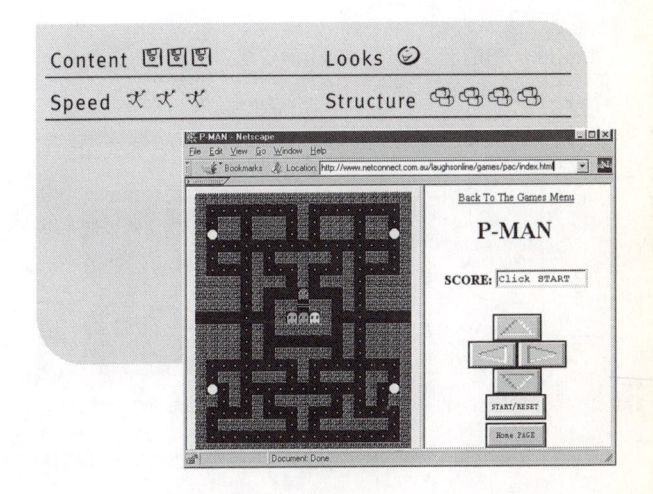

Content 📖📖📖	Looks 😊
Speed � � �	Structure 🥨🥨🥨🥨

Win at Blackjack
http://games.2nd.net/cards.html

It's better than the real thing because you don't pay your PC when you lose. And you can beat the machine. It (the dealer) has to hit on 16 and stand on 17. The page links to four other card games: NetCell, Run 21 (a type of Solitaire), Slot Machine and Video Poker.

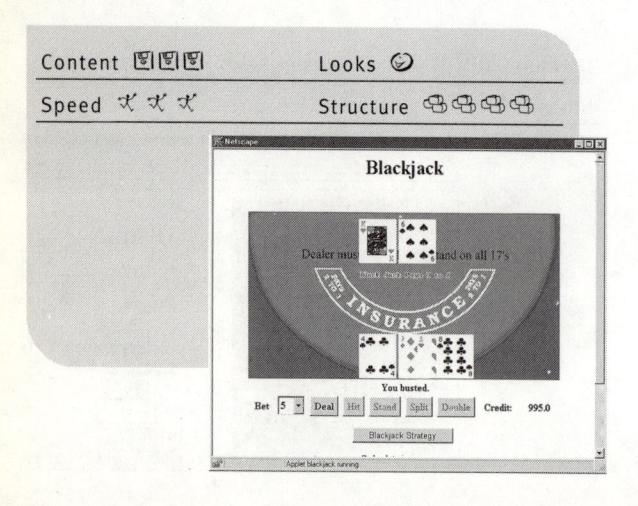

Content 📖📖📖	Looks ☺
Speed ✈✈✈	Structure 🐚🐚🐚🐚

Virtual crosswords
http://www.clevermedia.com/arcade/clevercrossword.html

Across: Australian acacia, Dutch name of the Hague. Down: Monetary unit of Vietnam, Soviet news service. These online crossword puzzles provide clues with varying degrees of difficulty. Save on ink, and collect hints if you're a cheat.

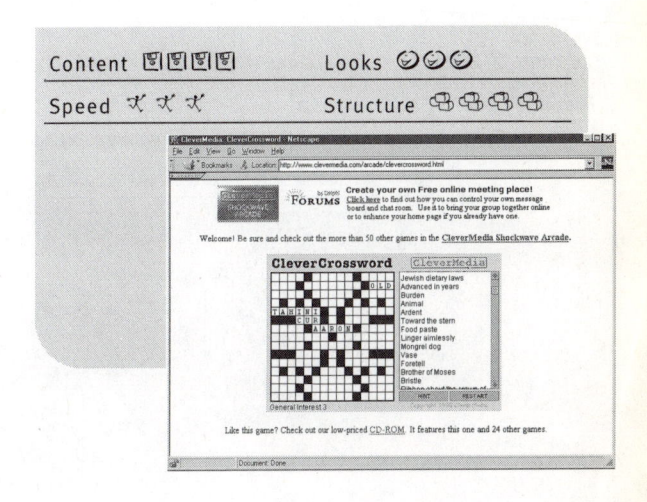

Content 📖📖📖📖   Looks 😊😊😊

Speed 🏃 🏃 🏃   Structure 🏛🏛🏛🏛

Your special subject is . . .

http://www.kipper.com/master.htm

There were two Mastermind games floating around in the 1970s. One was a television quiz show, but the one this site virtualises was a little hand-held memory game for two people involving coloured pegs and a series of rows of holes to line them up in. In the online version, one player has to guess the order of the virtual opponent's row of coloured pegs. Have a go.

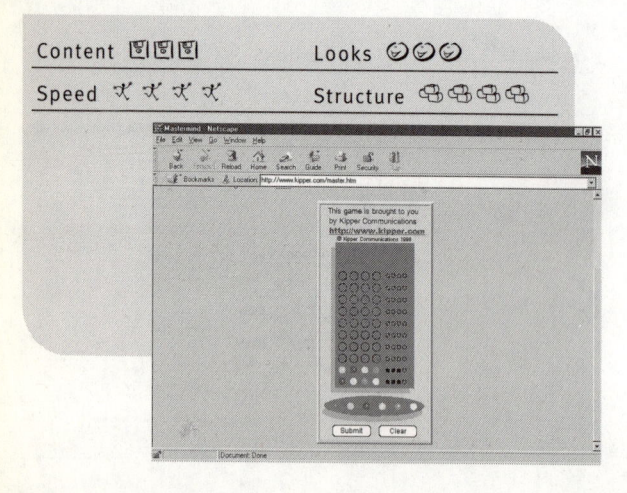

Content 📖📖📖	Looks 😊😊😊
Speed ✗ ✗ ✗ ✗	Structure 🕸🕸🕸🕸

Hackey sack
http://www.shockrave.com/members/games/archive/

The virtual hackey sack game you'll find among this list of archived Shockrave games is noisy but fun, just like the real thing. The collection is part of the Shockrave site, run by Macromedia, the people who brought Shockwave to the world, so the games make full use of the available technology. You could also try Aussie Surf Classic, 3D Tic Tac Toe or Shockrave's version of virtual Air Hockey.

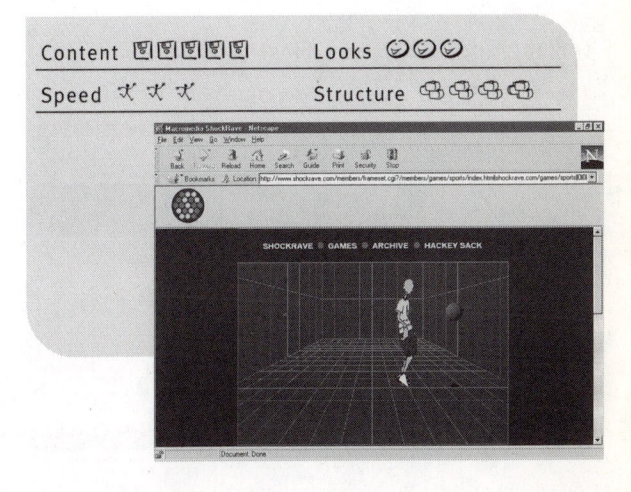

Content	👾👾👾👾	Looks	☺☺☺
Speed	✗✗✗	Structure	🐢🐢🐢🐢

Are you penguin enough?
http://www.hahnice.com.au/games/shootpen/

The Hahn Ice site will try to encourage you to buy more beer by offering visitors great games featuring cute little penguins. The Air Hockey Challenge shoot-'em-up game involves smashing bottles of Hahn Ice floating through a polar landscape. Try to be kind to the penguins: their eyes pop out of their skulls if you accidentally hit them instead of the bottle. The sound effects are great. A perfect antidote for those furies that make you feel like smashing bottles against the wall – throw a virtual tantrum instead.

Content	🍺🍺🍺🍺	Looks	😊😊😊😊😊
Speed	✶✶✶✶	Structure	🐧🐧🐧🐧

Wav.length

http://www.dailywav.com

'I want total sensory deprivation and backup drugs!' says Jennifer Saunders in *Absolutely Fabulous*. The Daily.WAV is the world's greatest time waster. Wander through its archives and listen to television, film and radio sound files that can fill lonely hours, bring back golden memories and always raise a smile (how's that for schmaltzy?). It's a seriously fun place to visit, though. Which of the following would you prefer to hear in bed tonight: 'Isn't that what being an international man of mystery is all about?' (Mike Myers from *Austin Powers*) or 'Here's looking at you, kid' (Humphrey Bogart from *Casablanca*)?

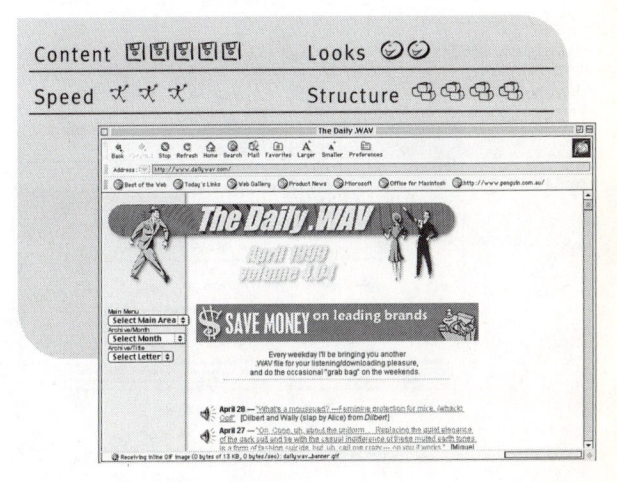

Content 📼📼📼📼📼   Looks 😊😊

Speed ✈ ✈ ✈   Structure 🏰🏰🏰🏰

TV and movie soundbytes
http://wso.williams.edu/~mgarland/sounds/

Listen to clips from *Psycho*, *Jaws*, *Beverly Hills Cop* and *Mission: Impossible* or to the *James Bond* theme. Then reminisce to the theme songs from *CHiPs*, *Charles in Charge*, *Doogie Howser MD*, *Fraggle Rock*, *I Dream of Jeannie*, *The Incredible Hulk*, *Mr Ed*, *M*A*S*H*, *The Six Million Dollar Man*, *The Wonder Years*, *The X-Files* and dozens more.

Content 📖📖📖📖📖	Looks 😊😊
Speed ✈ ✈ ✈	Structure 🌀🌀🌀🌀🌀

The absolutely incredible counting page

http://www.littlejason.com/autocount.html

You'd have to be really bored to spend any serious length of time here, but it's worth a visit. It's a page that the Count from *Sesame Street* would love. The counter just keeps on turning over, before your eyes. Go away for a week, then come back to see how much counting the page has done in your absence. Why? Well, you see, the Web is just a weird and wild place.

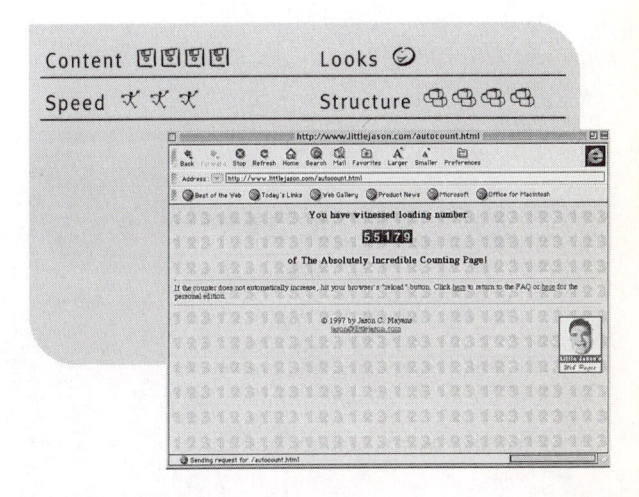

Content 📖📖📖📖	Looks 😊
Speed ✈✈✈	Structure ⊕⊕⊕⊕

The dialectizer

http://www.rinkworks.com/dialect/

This crazy site rewrites text into other dialects. We ran the *Herald* site through it at one stage, changing 'HE'S BACK! Champion spinner Shane Warne is tweaking at the crease again' to the redneck 'HE'S BACK! Fry mah hide! Champion spinner Shane Warne is tweakin' at th' crease agin'. In Swedish chef dialect, he's 'tveekeeng et zee creese-a egeeen. Bork bork bork!' Test your pig Latin and translate this headline: '*Epublicansray inyay urmoiltay asyay Ingrichgay itsquay*'.

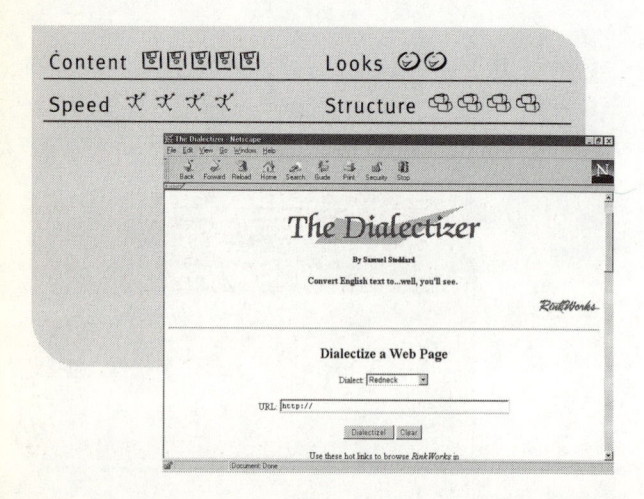

Content 🗿🗿🗿🗿🗿   Looks 😊😊
Speed ✈✈✈✈   Structure ♧♧♧♧

Push my buttons
http://members.aol.com/INVIEGLE/funnyfaces.html

A site for compulsive people. It's a really silly way to waste five minutes, but also a really clever way of using the Web's best attributes. It starts out with a warping Bill Clinton, but becomes a journey through the pages of a site that contain what must be the only button on the face of the earth with a personality. It even attempts to lure you away from the task of pushing its buttons by asking whether you're hungry (and putting the words *pizza pizza* in the mouseover text box – make sure you read those mouseovers).

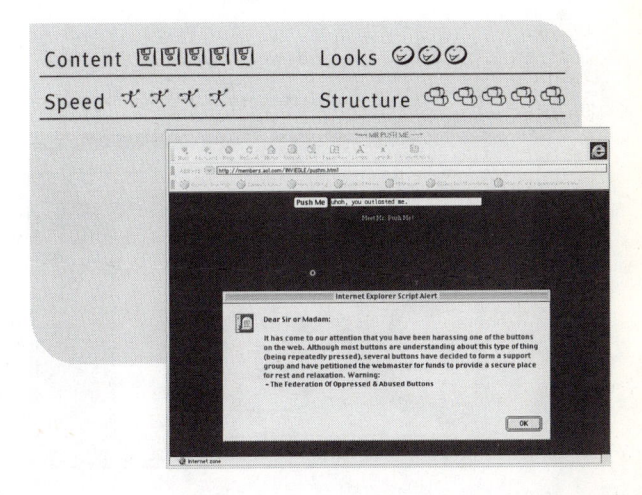

Be nice to real dogs, but laugh at this
http://www.word.com/thething/pieces/microwave/

An amusing and sad Web game. Putting the cute animated dog into the virtual microwave seems harmless enough. Setting the timer for 10 seconds makes him shake a little, but he's OK. Twenty seconds sends him into more of a spin. Thirty seconds . . . Click. Bowooom. Aaaarrrghhhh . . . I feel guilty. Never, ever, ever try this at home.

Content 🖳🖳🖳🖳	Looks 😊😊😊
Speed ✯✯✯	Structure 🍪🍪🍪🍪

Snooty

http://www.snoot.com

Who needs friends when you've got Snoot? Here's a site that will provide you with hours of entertainment. Try Choose Your Own Schizophrenia. It's like that game where you write part of a story on a piece of paper, then pass it to the next player to add his or her piece, except that the site adds the next piece, then gives you another choice. Snoot's poll questions include the scary 'Are you good or evil?' Thirty-three per cent of respondents claimed to be evil. The whole thing is accessorised by a collection of little blue characters called snoots.

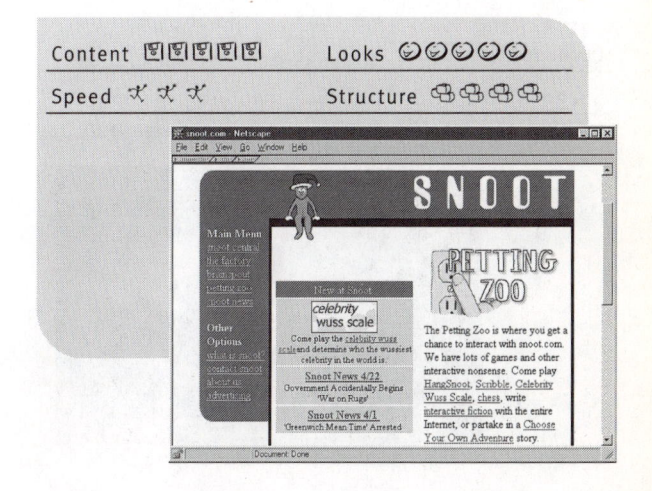

Content 📖📖📖📖 Looks 😊😊😊😊
Speed ✼ ✼ ✼ Structure 🌀🌀🌀🌀

Superfro

http://www.toyota.com.au/superfro/superfro.html

Apart from the fact that you have to collect lucky Toyota medallions to help your 'fro to grow, you can have so much fun playing this sexy little number that you forget it's a glorified piece of Webvertising. A groovy beat pumps on in the background as you collect the medallions. Or use a magic comb to shield yourself from UFO rays and flying cheese fondue pots. Bizarre.

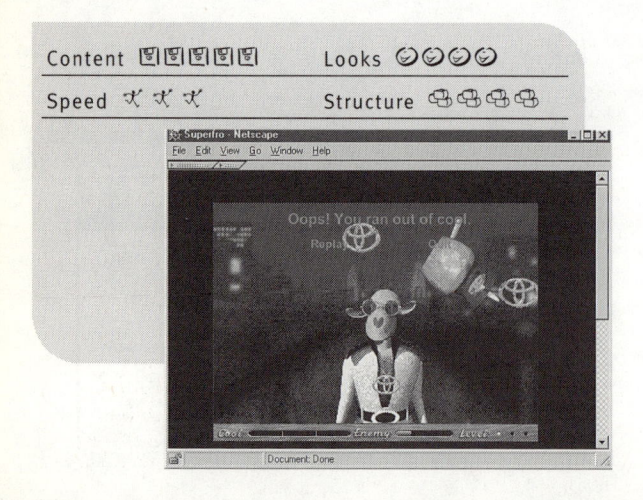

Content	🎖🎖🎖🎖🎖	Looks	😊😊😊😊
Speed	✻✻✻	Structure	♧♧♧♧

Virtual bubble wrap
http://fathom.org/opalcat/virtualbw.html

We recommend extensive use of bubble wrap when giving presents, particularly to anyone under the age of ten. That's a blatant lie, actually. We recommend bubble wrap for EVERYONE. We ALL love popping those tantalisingly poppable clear plastic pockets of air. This web site is the next best thing. You won't find any presents there, but you can virtually pop to your heart's content.

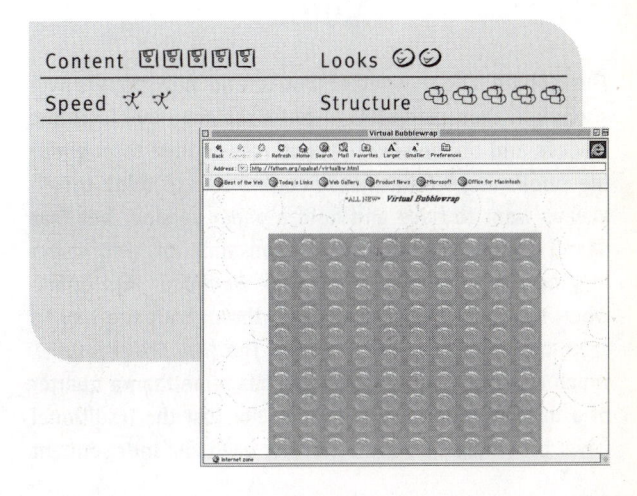

Content 📕📕📕📕📕   Looks 😊😊

Speed ✗ ✗   Structure 🌀🌀🌀🌀🌀

two

Media

The debate about whether books and newspapers will survive in their current form or be replaced by electronic devices and online services continues to rage throughout the publishing world. Most people seem to think they'll always want to have and hold a paper version, but that hasn't stopped hundreds of thousands of Web users logging onto the *Sydney Morning Herald* or *Age* online when they first get to work, and throughout the day to catch up on breaking news stories. The *Wall Street Journal*, which charges a subscription fee, has more than a quarter of a million online users. But it's not just the traditional news providers that are attracting eyeballs. Independent publishers have carved strong niche markets by going online. *Geekgirl*, for example, uses plenty of multimedia and interactivity to encourage return visits, as do the newspaper sites. That's the beauty of the online media. It's not just print or audio or video or graphics or an online forum – it's the lot. And because it's so easy for someone to set up a site, and because you can access information from anywhere in the world, you can always find a site to suit your interest. The fact is, you can probably type in the name of any major newspaper, magazine, television network or radio station in the western world and find a site.

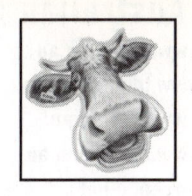

Australian media

http://www.smh.com.au
http://www.theage.com.au
http://www.afr.com.au
http://www.news.com.au
http://www.abc.net.au
http://www.ninemsn.com.au

The strength of Australian news sites lies in their indexes in a topic area, such as the *Herald*'s collection of stories and links on Clinton's impeachment. They also provide up-to-date in-depth coverage of breaking news from various agencies, and point users to primary sources and other related links. Users can catch up with news on any subject, at any time of the day, from anywhere in the world. They allow you to print out longer stories to file away, read on the train or send to a friend.

The ABC's breaking news service is the best of the lot. ABC Online can access the broadcaster's national and international radio and television networks' updates. At this stage, Ninemsn, News Ltd and Fairfax daytime updates mostly rely on wire copy from the same source, AAP. There are some exceptions, such as major sporting events and elections, where Web-dedicated journalists will file copy and/or audio or video grabs specifically for the online audience.

There's more to a good media site than news, of course. Dig deep into the ABC site to find The Lab, their brilliant science section. The *Herald*'s Icon section includes a weekly reader poll, useful tutorials, and sends you straight to the week's most interesting and pertinent web sites. The *Australian*'s site, which you'll find at the **news.com.au** address, will deliver Net News to your inbox daily. Ninemsn features daily astrology updates, live chats with Channel Nine stars, great games and a virtual reading group within *HQ* Online.

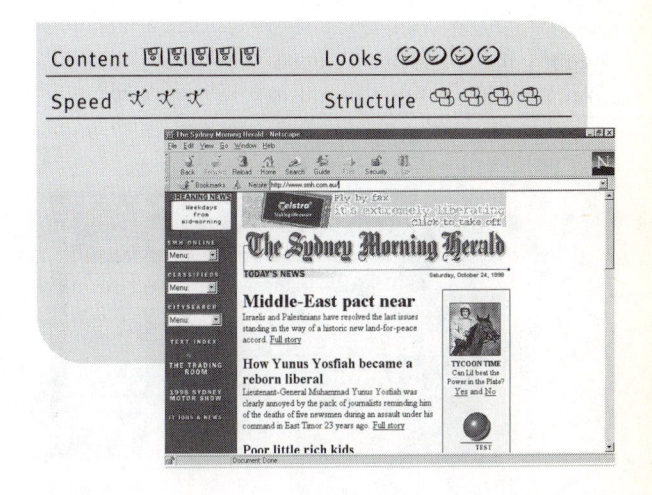

British media

http://www.bbc.co.uk
http://www.beeb.com

The BBC site pops up on most English expats' lists of favourite sites, and not only for its brilliant news coverage. Stop by for a chat about the influence of Earl Spencer on Simon's speech at Tiffany's funeral in *EastEnders*; read about Egg and Milly's romantic dilemmas in *This Life*; or explore the alien fact file in the *Doctor Who* site. Click on through to **beeb.com**, which is a crazy but fun and incredibly racy-looking collection of BBC-branded Web zines.

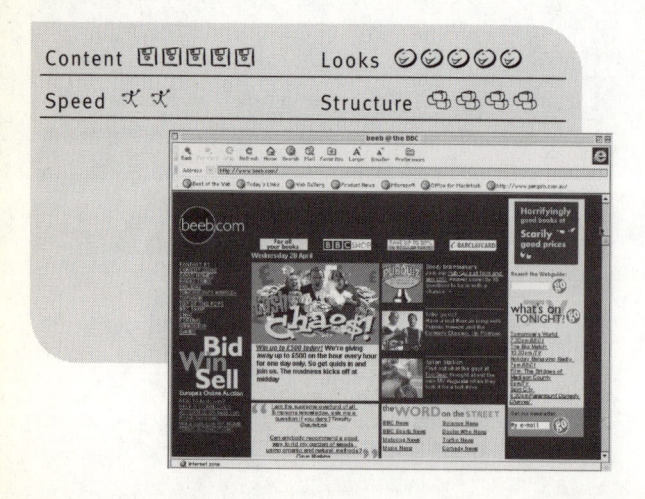

Content 📖📖📖📖	Looks 😊😊😊😊😊
Speed ✈ ✈	Structure 🗂🗂🗂🗂

American media

http://www.nyt.com

The *New York Times* site made my day when it dropped subscription charges altogether in 1998. These days, once you've registered, you can read some of the world's best journalism every day for nix.

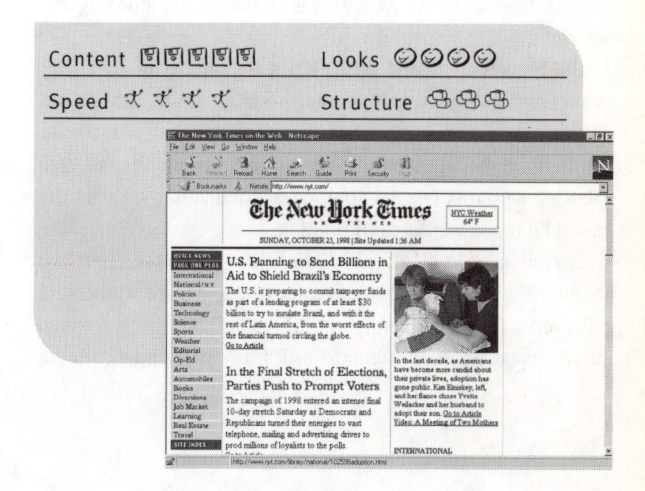

Content 📖📖📖📖📖   Looks 😊😊😊😊

Speed ✈ ✈ ✈ ✈   Structure 🕸🕸🕸

Web-only media

http://www.wired.com/news/
http://www.news.com
http://www.tabloid.net
http://www.theonion.com
http://www.salonmagazine.com

Web-only media groups often provide better online news coverage than the old hands because their sites have been developed from scratch. In contrast, TV, radio and print media are primarily about taking television, radio or print content, redesigning it, changing it a little, and publishing it in another context, that is, on the Web (this is known as 'repurposing' the content).

CNET's **news.com** and *Wired* News are among the best sites for Internet and general technology-related news. *Tabloid* is a virtual publication that takes a cynical look at the stories mainstream media is publishing around the world; the Web allows the journalists to compile a publication without the added financial pressures of printing.

Speaking of cynical, *The Onion* is a must-see. Here's a sample: 'NEW YORK: *Cosmopolitan* writer Melissa Rutherford achieved a journalistic milestone Tuesday, when she cranked out the magazine's 10 billionth article revealing how to bring out the animal in your man. "Surprise him by greeting him after work in a sexy new red cocktail dress," wrote drained, numb Rutherford, who has advised *Cosmopolitan* readers how to bring out the animal in their men 135 285 times during her six-year tenure with the magazine.'

On a more serious note, *Salon* is a quality online journal. Its feature writers and columnists provide some of the best food for thought on the Web.

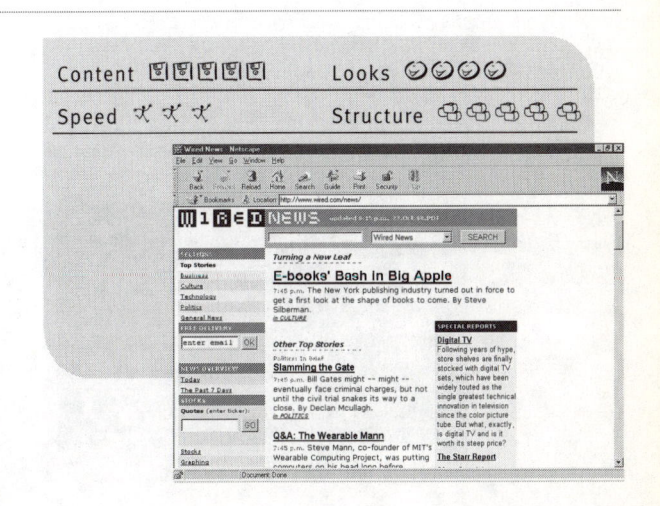

Urban films
http://www.urbancinefile.com.au

Andrew Urban, famous in SBS viewing circles for his fabulous *Front Up* vox-pop program, also runs (with Louise Keller) a web site filled with film facts. The Cinefile runs loads of video and movie-ticket giveaways, holds openings, and generally lets the film buff know what's happening as it happens. The section that lists films by opening date is a great resource.

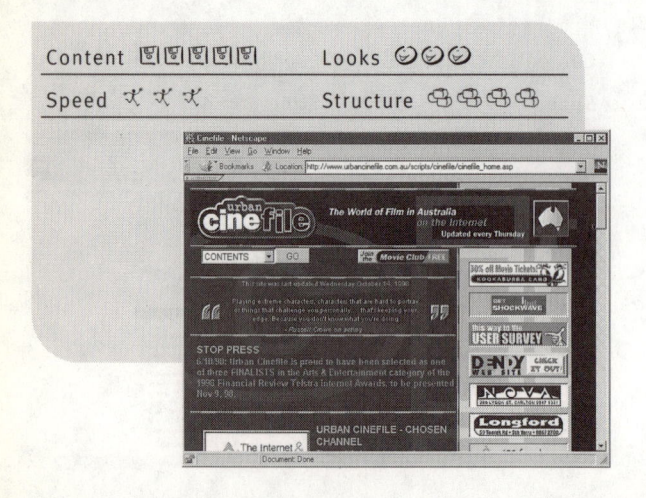

Content	📖📖📖📖📖	Looks	😊😊😊
Speed	✈✈✈	Structure	🏗🏗🏗🏗

Vote for your favourite song
http://www.abc.net.au/triplej/net50/vote.htm

National youth radio network Triple J has a hip web site that ties in with their Saturday night radio schedule. Visit and choose your favourite (or least favourite) tracks with your mouse during the week, then hear them played back on the Net 50 each Saturday. You have the choice of clicking on a track in their list online, or entering one that you've come up with independently.

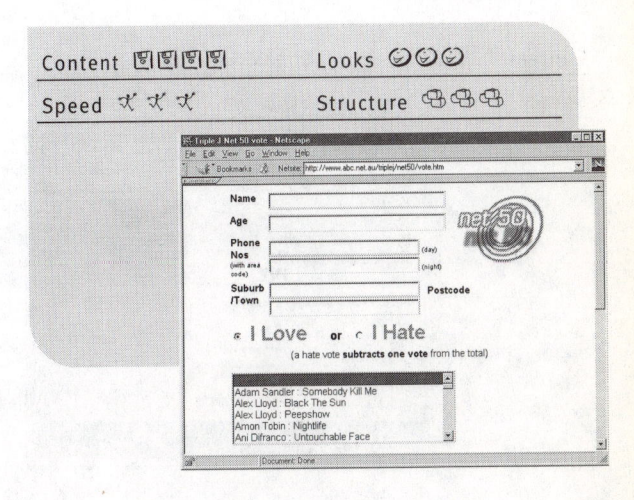

Content 🖼️🖼️🖼️🖼️   Looks ☺☺☺

Speed ✈ ✈ ✈   Structure ⊕⊕⊕

Geek chicks
http://www.geekgirl.com.au

Geekgirl is the matriarch of Australian web sites, having reigned over the ether since 1995. It describes itself as 'the bi-monthly e-zine for groovers' and 'the world's first cyberfem Webzine', and promotes the tagline 'Grrls need modems'. That's important, because the Net has from time to time had a for-nerdy-little-boys-only image. Anti-nerd chicks like it too. Check out the SPRACI section (Sydney Party Rave and Club Information), e-cards, digital art, Shockwave games, link-filled columns on media, the arts and technology, an eclectic mix of features and geekgrrrlish news.

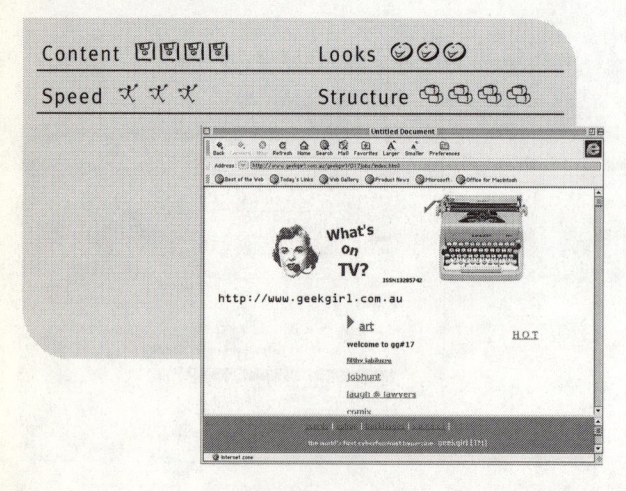

Content 🖫🖫🖫🖫	Looks ☺☺☺
Speed ✄ ✄ ✄	Structure ⊛⊛⊛⊛

Louder and louder

http://www.loud.net.au

LOUD, the biannual youth culture, arts and media festival, is funded by the Australia Council and was first held in January 1998. The best creative work of Australia's youth infiltrated all media, from art, drama, television, radio and film to zines, newspapers, magazines and the Web. The site was HUGE as well as LOUD. It's all archived, so take a look at some amazing online comic books, e-zines, Web theatre and film, digital art, postcards and photography, or follow links to some of the best Australian youth-run sites.

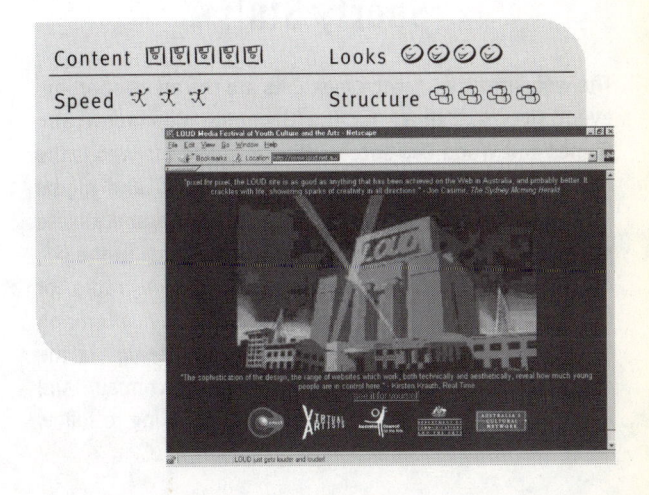

Content 📖📖📖📖📖	Looks ☺☺☺☺
Speed ✄ ✄ ✄	Structure 🐢🐢🐢🐢

three

Sporty Stuff

The web sites that get the megahits are the mega-sporting-event sites like those for the Olympics, Commonwealth Games and World Cup soccer. Why? Because the Web is the perfect medium for providing instant scores and medal updates alongside easily searchable statistics and athlete profiles. It's fantastic for when you're overseas; in the US, for instance, you'll have trouble finding a radio or television station broadcasting a Saturday afternoon AFL game, but you can keep up with your team via the *Age*'s live text-based coverage (www.footy99.com.au). And if you're in Malaysia for a business trip but dying to follow the Bledisloe Cup matches, you can, because there's a Rugby site that blasts live audio coverage to the world. When video improves, we'll be watching Pat Rafter win the US Open in the top left-hand corner of our computer screens while we work (although most of the big sporting events have sold television rights to networks so that even official web sites are devoid of live video – damnation). Even the smallest sporting club in the smallest town playing the most obscure sport can post its results, team lists and photos online.

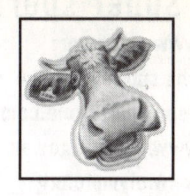

Super sports sites

http://www.cnnsi.com
http://cbs.sportsline.com
http://espn.sportszone.com
http://www.ausport.gov.au
http://www.olympic.org
http://www.sydney.olympic.org

Sports fans, start your Web tour here. The mega American sports sites are so big and comprehensive, it's a wonder any of the smaller sites survive. If you're not into basketball, baseball or American football, you might find them tedious at first glance, but look beyond the balls, because CNNSI, Sportsline and ESPN Sportszone are great news and stats resources. They cover every internationally recognised sport you can think of using text, photos, audio, video, interactive games and more. Try their special sites for major tournaments and finals series – they're often better than the official sites.

While it's not terribly glamorous, the Australian Sports Commission site provides information on just about every sport played here, from fencing to polo.

As the Sydney 2000 Games near, interest in the Olympic movement can be divided between sports and event fans who can't get enough, cynics who can't wait to get out of the country while it's on, and journalists who thrive on the inevitable political quagmire surrounding it. For sports fans, the important thing is knowing what's on where and when, who wins gold, and in what time or with what score. The major Sydney media sites will all provide comprehensive coverage, some in conjunction with global partners. The official site, which will undoubtedly be the most-hit web site in history, will provide the vital instantaneous results, plus photos, multimedia, interactivity, news, features and previews galore.

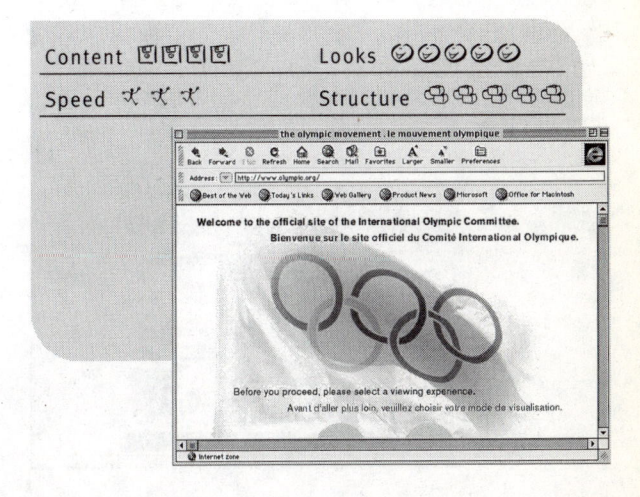

Content 🖻🖻🖻🖻   Looks ☺☺☺☺

Speed ✧ ✧ ✧   Structure 🏛🏛🏛🏛🏛

the olympic movement . le mouvement olympique

Address: http://www.olympic.org/

Welcome to the official site of the International Olympic Committee.
Bienvenue sur le site officiel du Comité International Olympique.

Before you proceed, please select a viewing experience.
Avant d'aller plus loin, veuillez choisir votre mode de visualisation.

Hockey one, hockey two

http://www.ausport.gov.au/wha/
http://www.FIHockey.org

Though Australia's men's and women's hockey teams are respectively close to the best and absolutely the best in the world, hockey tends to receive about as much media coverage as a game of marbles in this country. During the 1998 World Cup, one of the free-to-air television networks paid for the rights but didn't air a single game in full. Not even the women's final, which Australia won. Fortunately, the Fédération Internationale de Hockey site will keep you posted.

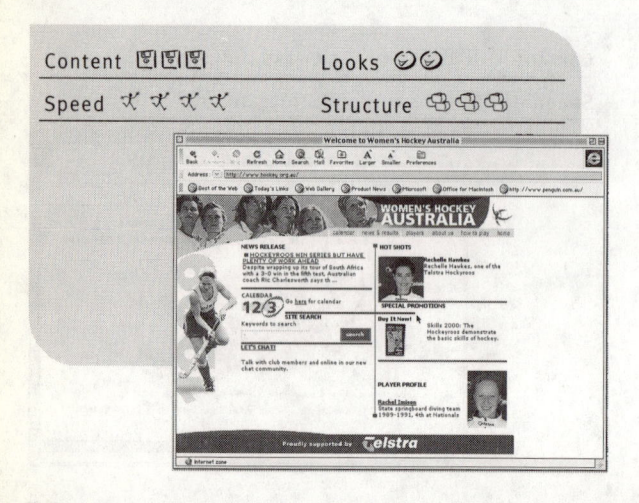

Content 🖺🖺🖺	Looks 😊😊
Speed ✗ ✗ ✗ ✗	Structure 🌀🌀🌀

Squash vital people

http://www.squash.org

Our squash players are the quieter achievers of Australian sport. The Internet Squash Federation is a good place to find out more about the game, including world rankings. The top two women are Aussies Sarah FitzGerald and Michelle Martin, while our Rodney Eyles, a former number two, is ranked fourth in the world. FitzGerald says the squash world is 'the same as the tennis scene; just take three zeroes off the prize money'.

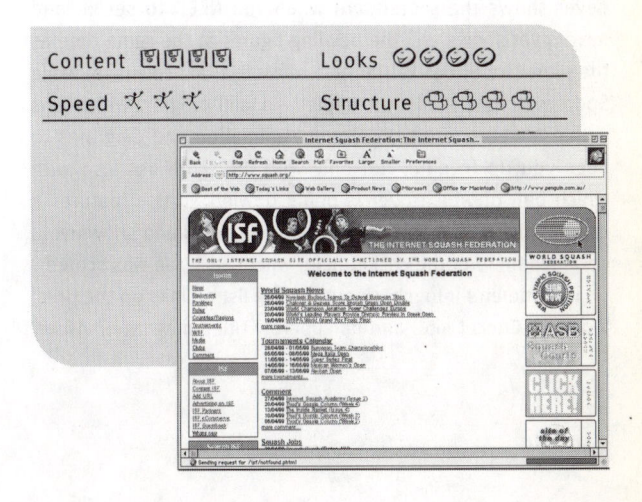

Content	Looks
Speed	Structure

Howzat?

http://www.cricket.org
http://www.cricket.fairfax.com.au
http://www.sportswatch.com.au
http://users.ox.ac.uk/~beth/wca.htm
http://www.ausport.gov.au/wca/

Is cricket our national sport? If you're a fan, you probably already know about these sites. CricInfo, at the top of the list, provides an international perspective on the game, including a daily email newsletter. Its scoreboards are live and comprehensive, which is very important, because Richie Benaud never shows the scoreboard when you NEED to see it, and never ever shows you the bowling figures at the same time as the scorecard either. Fairfax also offers live text coverage, while Sportswatch's matchlet (or 'applet' – a mini-program which runs within a web site) uses colourful animation and diagrams to keep you up to date, not only with the score but also with which ball of which over is being bowled. It also features a comparative line graph of each team's innings and shows you, on a mini-map of the cricket field, where each run was scored.

For women's info, check out the big list of links on the Brits' Women's Cricket site, and its superbly titled magazine, *Wicket*

Women. Or take a look at the Aussie women's cricket site, where the national team are pictured on the Balcony at Lord's following their 5–0 victory over England in July 1998. Unfortunately, their green-and-gold pyjama uniform is no better than the men's. I blame Kerry Packer.

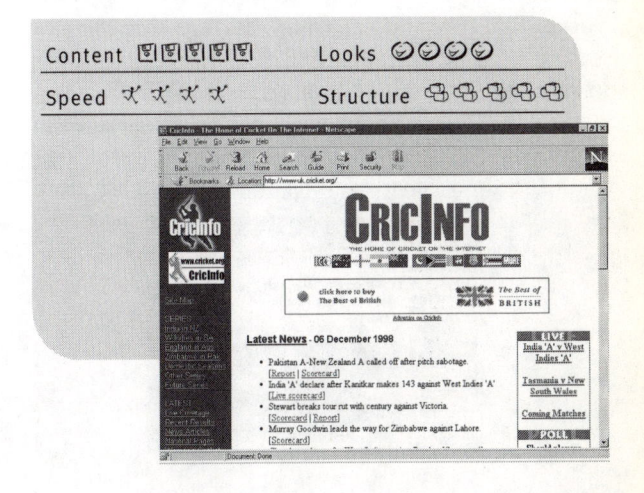

Content 📖📖📖📖 Looks ☺☺☺☺

Speed 🏏🏏🏏🏏 Structure 🏉🏉🏉🏉🏉

Fever pitch

http://www.soccernet.com
http://www.fifa.com
http://ozsoccer.thehub.com.au

For all the latest official international soccer info, try FIFA (Fédération Internationale de Football Association). If you're a homesick Pom, visit Soccernet. Its coverage of the Premier League and FA Cup is among the best you'll find online. If you're interested in what's happening in Aussie soccer, try – you guessed it – Ozsoccer.

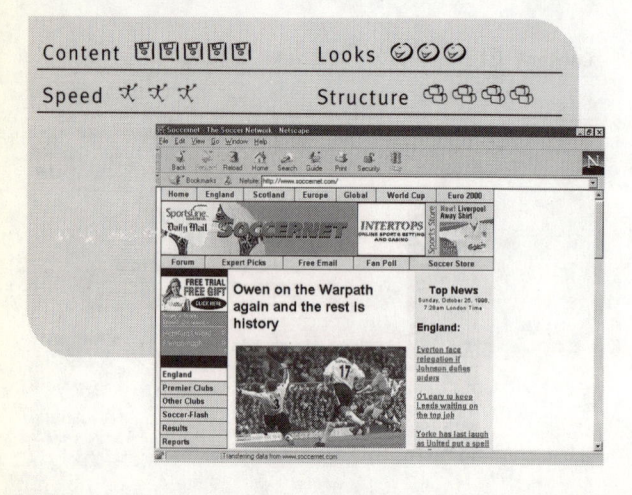

Content 📺📺📺📺 Looks ☺☺☺
Speed ✈✈✈ Structure 🐠🐠🐠🐠

Part of the Union

http://www.rugby.com.au
http://www.rugbyheaven.com

The official Australian Rugby Union site includes a section on the Wallaroos (they're the rugger women), but rugby heaven is the place to be for Rugby info online. It's a joint effort developed by the *Sydney Morning Herald*, the *New Zealand Herald* and the Independent Online group from South Africa. And it *is* heaven for rugby fans.

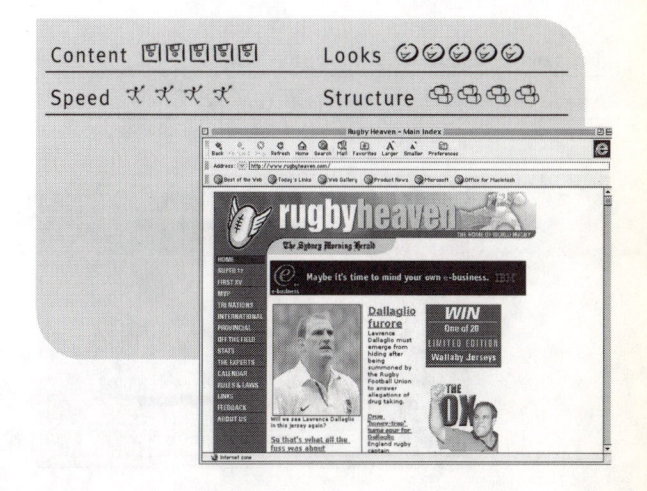

Content 📖📖📖📖📖   Looks 😊😊😊😊😊
Speed ✕ ✕ ✕ ✕   Structure 🥨🥨🥨🥨

Try these

http://www.nrl.com.au
http://www.eisa.net.au/~pbrand/

The National Rugby League seems to have settled down again in the wake of Super League. The official site, on the other hand, seems to come and go depending on resources, marketing strategy or whim. If it is there, you'll find draws, team profiles and links to team sites. If it's not, try the Insane Sports National Rugby League site. It invites users to 'sign me guest book', 'see which games are been showed on TV' [sic] and click through team lists, the draw, a chatroom, news, links, results and the ladder.

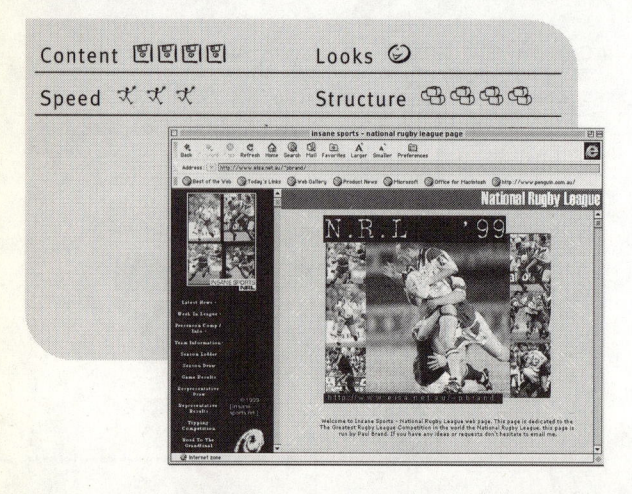

Content 📖📖📖📖	Looks 🙂
Speed ✈ ✈ ✈	Structure 🐌🐌🐌🐌

Aussie rules, OK?

http://www.footy99.com.au
http://www.afl.com.au

If you're an AFL fan, you'll be jumping for joy when you see Footy 99's Aussie Rules coverage. As well as a massive site including live, mark-by-mark text coverage of every game, they offer an email newsletter to keep fans up to speed on match reports and analysis, injury reports, stats, betting information and news. In 2000, the address will be **www.footy2000.com.au**. The official AFL site, which is a joint venture between the AFL, the Seven Network and News Ltd, provides audio and video coverage of some games.

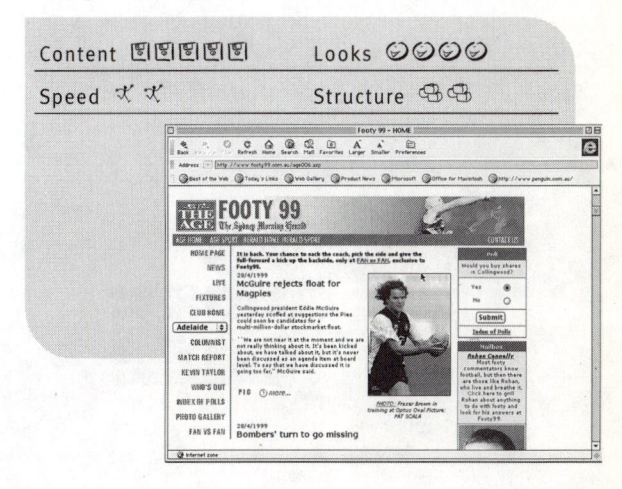

Content 📖📖📖📖	Looks ☺☺☺☺
Speed ✈ ✈	Structure 🐌🐌

Goal attack

http://www.netball.asn.au
http://www.cobweb.com.au/~kathardel/

Get on the ball with the Netball Australia site. Netball has the fourth-highest participation rate of any sport or physical activity in this country (after aerobics, golf and tennis), which is impressive when you consider that not many men play. The official site is cheery, newsy and useful. Read up on techniques, print out a calendar of events or the Commonwealth Bank Trophy draw, or order videos and rule books. Then switch to Elizabeth's Australian Netball Gallery, a fantastic fanzine featuring profiles, photos, links, quizzes and an email newsletter.

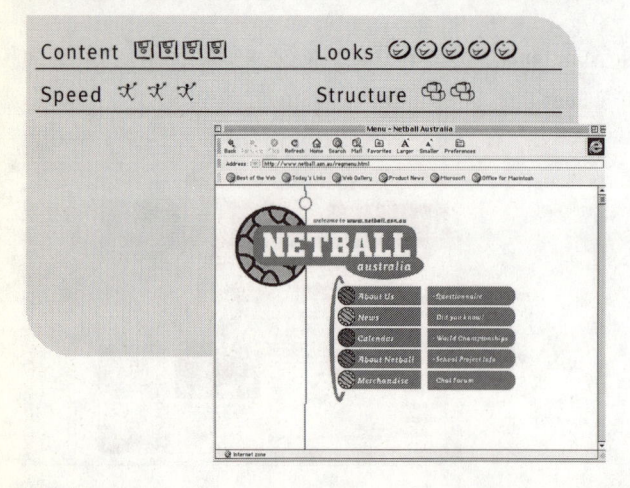

Content 📖📖📖📖	Looks 😊😊😊😊😊
Speed 🏃🏃🏃	Structure 🧩🧩

Slam dunks

http://www.basketball.net.au
http://www.nbltoday.waus.net

The official Basketball Australia site is one of the most comprehensive sports sites I've ever seen. Its table of contents is mind-boggling, listing all the national and local teams, tournament dates and results, where to play, contacts, recruitment details, international organisations, wheelchair basketball associations, coaching tips and star profiles. Also visit NBL Today, an unofficial site which is updated daily.

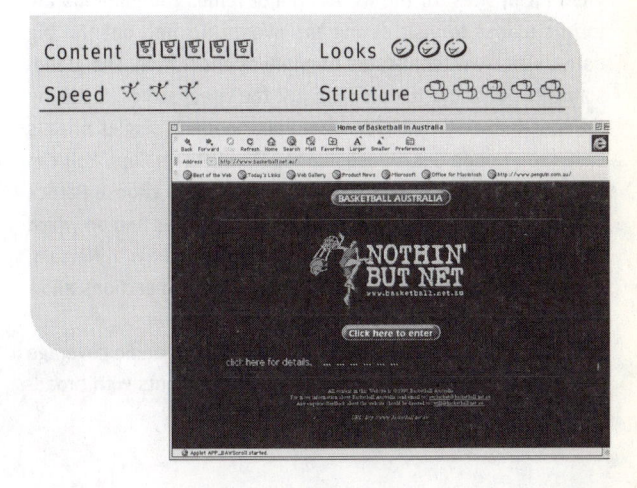

Content 🖺🖺🖺🖺   Looks 😊😊😊
Speed 🏃🏃🏃   Structure 🏀🏀🏀🏀🏀

Serve an ace

http://www.itftennis.com
http://www.wimbledon.org
http://www.frenchopen.org
http://www.usopen.org
http://www.ausopen.org
http://www.daviscup.org
http://www.worldtennisratings.com
http://www.tennisaustralia.com.au
http://www.corelwtatour.com
http://www.atptour.com

The official sites for the world's major tennis tournaments are terrific places to visit during the events. To find out the big dates, visit **www.tennistours.com/info/calender.html**. The grand-slam sites offer much more than just the latest scores, including the little-known French Open fact that the men's singles prize is called the Coupe des Mousquetaires (Musketeers Cup). You can also send an e-postcard to any of the players (I choose Patrick Rafter); find out exactly who's playing whom when and on which court; read feature articles; check out centre court with Netcam; and learn the events' histories. The merchandise sections allow you to order tennis paraphernalia online.

Some of the official tournament sites run live audio coverage of some matches, depending on rights agreements with broadcasters. And Fairfax (**www.theage.com.au** or **www.smh.com.au**) runs live text coverage of the Australian Open. The only thing that's lacking is live video coverage of the games, but hopefully in time demand will lead to television networks on-selling their highlights packages and live footage of the finals.

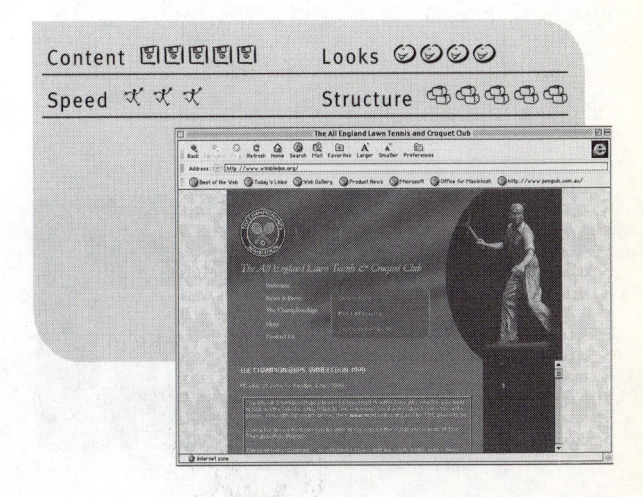

Content 🖺🖺🖺🖺🖺   Looks 😊😊😊😊

Speed ✗ ✗ ✗   Structure ♛♛♛♛♛

They're off!

http://www.ozracing.net.au
http://www.ajc.org.au
http://www.tabcorp.com.au

Some of us are strictly one-horse-race racing enthusiasts, so it's not surprising that Ozracing gives the Melbourne Cup and related Spring Carnival frivolity plenty of coverage each year. If you're a more-than-once-a-year-in-November flutterer, find out the quickest way to place a bet with the Tabcorp site, or check out the Australian Jockey Club site to find out what's on when and where.

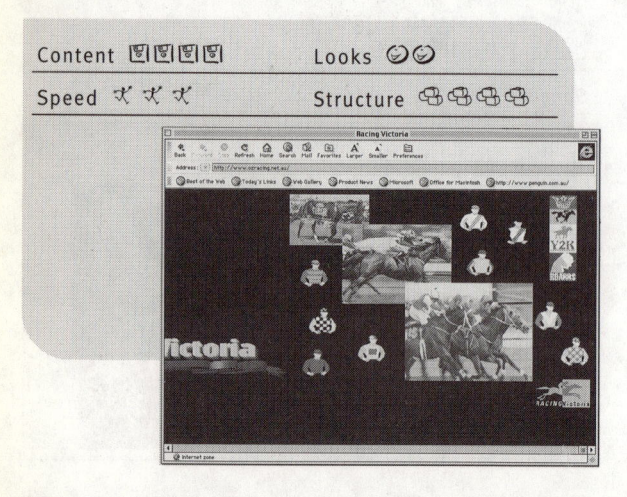

Content 🖫🖫🖫🖫	Looks ☺☺
Speed ✰✰✰	Structure 🐸🐸🐸🐸

Putt-putt time

http://19thhole.com
http://www.golfweb.com
http://www.pgatour.com

Golf is up there with aerobics at the top of the top ten participation sports, games and physical activities in Australia, so it's not surprising to find zillions of web sites designed to help you improve your game, choose a new set of clubs or follow the millionaires who play it professionally as they putt around the place. The 19th Hole site even has a section on how to take good golf photographs.

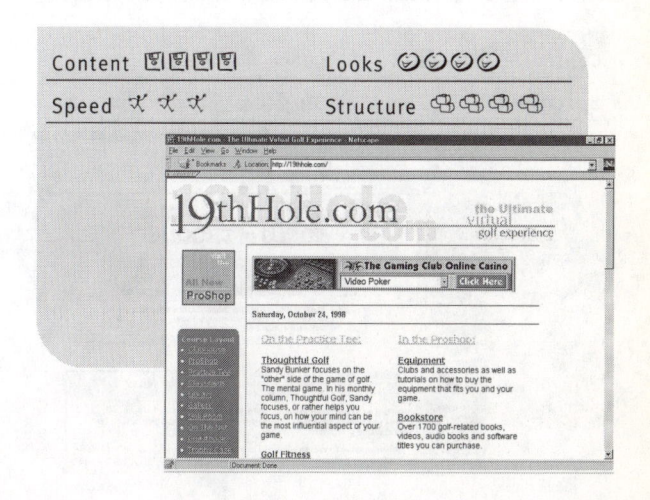

Content	📖📖📖📖	Looks	☺☺☺☺
Speed	✈✈✈	Structure	🕸🕸🕸🕸

Croquet and Pimms

http://www.croquet.com
http://www.ausport.gov.au/croqsp.html

Remember *Heathers*? Those bitchy, glamorous girls playing backyard croquet after school? They were on to a good thing. Bashing your mate's ball out of the way before pelting your own through the hoop is wild, particularly if you can pretend to be really posh and have cucumber sandwiches and Pimms between shots. Seriously though, croquet is a competitive sport played by all kinds of Australians. The Australian Sports Commission's croquet site will give you an insight into the local scene, while **croquet.com** offers an international perspective.

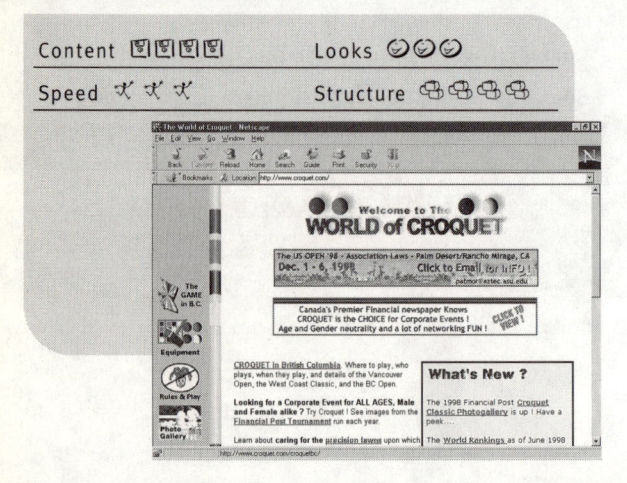

Content 🖳🖳🖳🖳	Looks ☺☺☺
Speed ↗↗↗	Structure ♋♋♋♋

Snow sports

http://www.ski.com.au
http://www.cyberski.com.au

Skiing fanatics will love the first-listed site, Sno-Info, especially its Webcams. More than a dozen cameras provide images of snow conditions every hour when ski lifts are in operation, at Charlotte Pass, Falls Creek, Mt Buffalo, Buller, Hotham, Selwyn, Thredbo, Perisher Blue, Baw Baw and Lake Mountain. The second site, Chill Factor, runs snow-sport features, photos, racing details, useful contacts, skier profiles, lift ticket prices and independent snow reports.

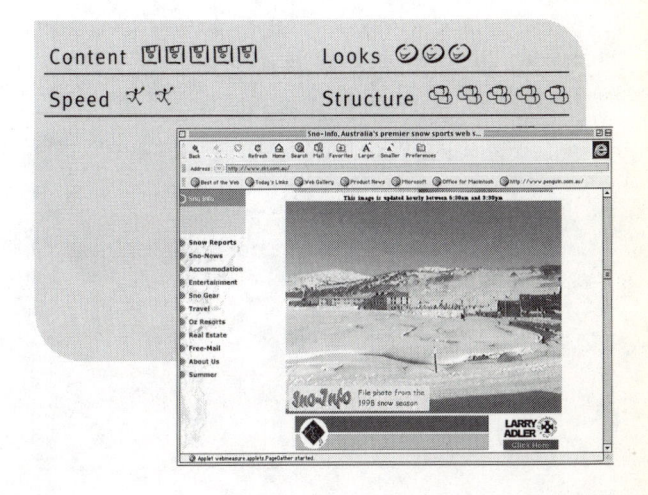

Hot-air ballooning history
http://www.ozemail.com.au/~pOgwil

The author of this site, Grahame Wilson, was bitten by the balloon bug many years ago: 'What other flying machine could grow from nothing, and then just sit there in complete silence?' The site includes 80 pictures and plenty of ballooning history. Grahame's flying career was cut short in 1981 when a hang-gliding accident left him a quadriplegic. He retired to put together this history and learnt how to build web sites, all from his wheelchair and with the use of only one hand.

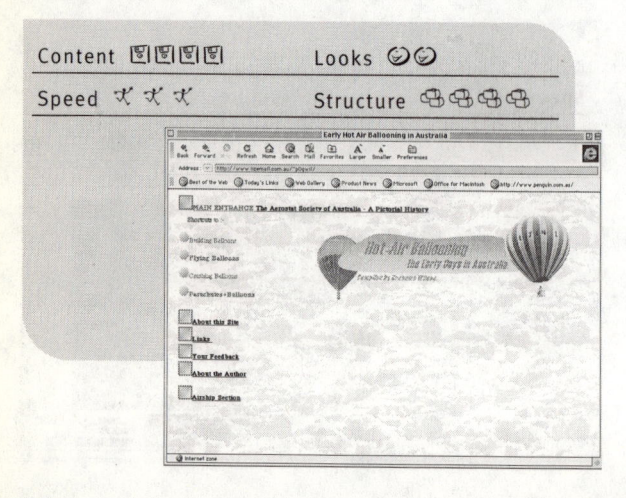

Content 😐😐😐😐	Looks 😊😊
Speed ✈ ✈ ✈	Structure 🎈🎈🎈🎈

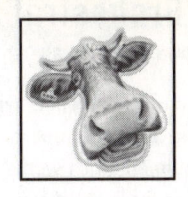

four

Music

This section is a bit of a mixed bag, because there are a lot of things you can do with music online. Having said that, the most frustrating thing that happened to me during the writing of this book was trying to find an audio clip of Pachelbel's 'Canon', my favourite piece of music. I was only able to find tinny-sounding electronic renditions. Erk! However, there are hundreds of radio sites constantly playing classical, jazz, rock, pop and folk music; news and magazine-style music sites combining multimedia with the *Rolling Stone*-style coverage of the music industry; sites that promote specific musicians; and sites that allow you to compose and play music for yourself.

Orchestral manoeuvres

http://www.aco.com.au

Classical music listeners will know the work of the Australian Chamber Orchestra, but may not be aware of their glamorous and multimedia-rich web site. It features a selection of audio grabs, the facility to buy tickets or CDs online via secure credit-card transaction, and a listing of performance dates for the next few months.

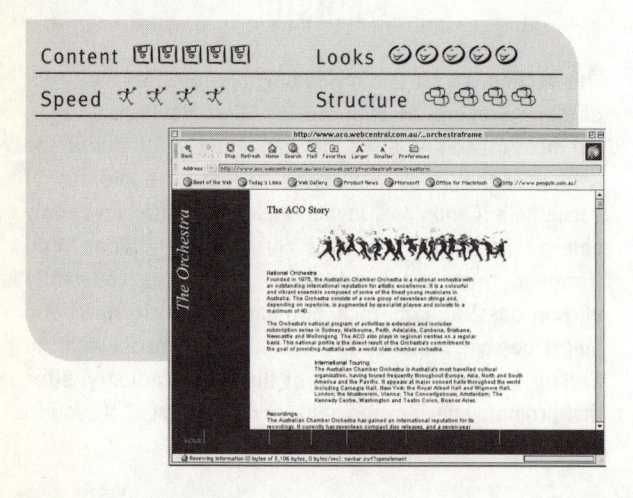

Content 📖📖📖📖📖   Looks 😊😊😊😊😊

Speed ✈ ✈ ✈ ✈   Structure 🔗🔗🔗🔗

For music addicts

http://www.addicted.com.au

Addicted to Noise is the Australian sister site of the more upmarket Sonicnet (see page 59). It is also a copycat of pioneering American online music zine **www.addicted.com**. The .au version features similar content to its predecessors, with an Australian slant. Try the random-access rock radio station, searchable archive of music and movie reviews, regular columnists, plus features and news.

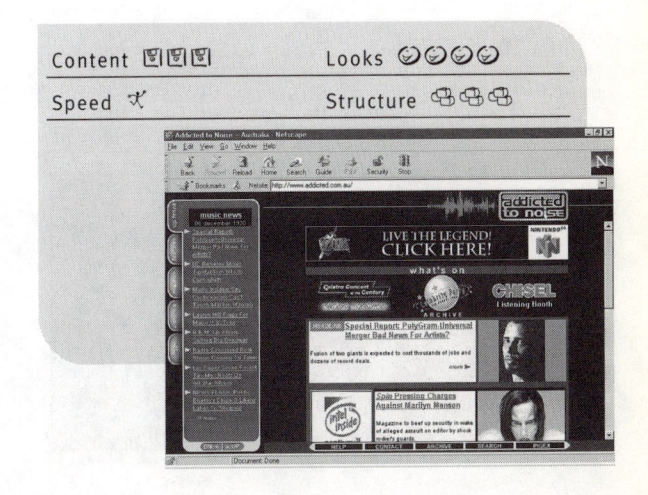

Content 📖📖📖	Looks 😊😊😊
Speed ✈	Structure 🐌🐌🐌

James Morrison, techno-head

http://www.jamesmorrison.com.au

You've probably seen James-Morrison-and-trumpet, but the sight of him fondling his IBM ThinkPad is techno-lust to the max. And when Australia's best-known jazz musician starts talking about how he spends hours window-shopping online for the latest gadget, you get the picture: this is a man who uses, understands and thrives on technology. His web site is testament to his understanding of the Net. It's turned Morrison Records into a 24-hour global shop, but better, because he is available to answer your questions online, or to join in huge Web-based jam sessions with musicians from around the world.

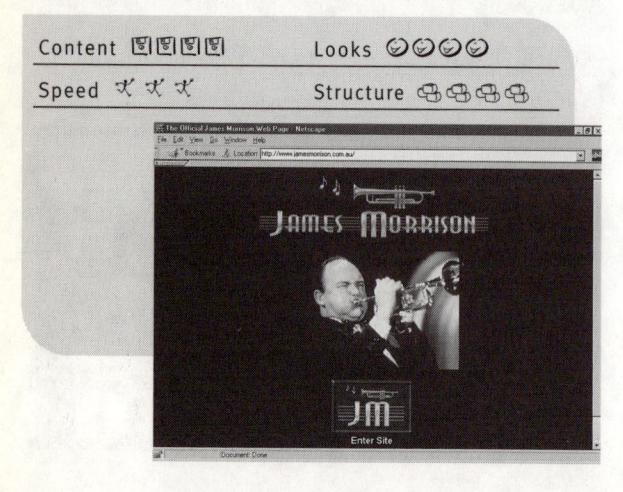

Content 📖📖📖📖	Looks 😊😊😊😊
Speed ✗ ✗ ✗	Structure ♧♧♧♧

Sonic boom

http://www.sonicnet.com

This American music site hits you in the face as soon as you arrive. The contents page is divided into daily news from around the world, a guide to the best music web sites, and live chats and cybercasts in The Station, alongside 24-hour channels offering music videos on demand. Make sure you run your mouse over the navigation buttons on the left-hand side of your screen, as there's a different sound attached to each. You can almost play your own music. The only thing I miss from an older version of Sonicnet is this quote: 'If you can't find something here to expand your horizons, go listen to Celine Dion.'

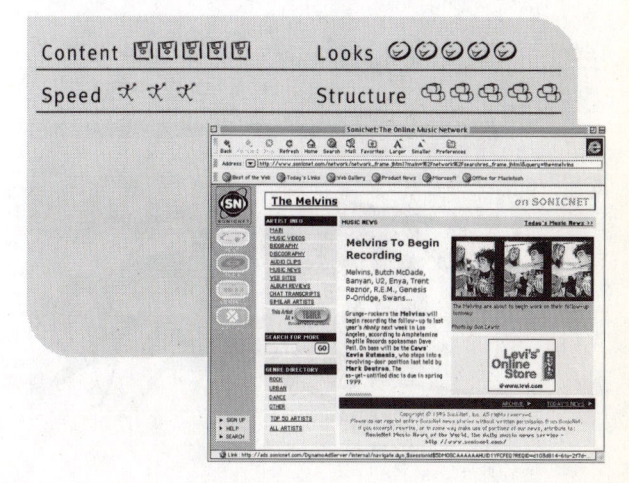

Content ▨▨▨▨▨   Looks ☺☺☺☺☺
Speed ✗ ✗ ✗   Structure ♘♘♘♘♘

Massive

http://www.massiveattack.co.uk

In what was probably a world first, Bristol pop trio Massive Attack Web-launched tracks, videos and artwork from their third album, *Mezzanine*, online. The band added previews each day during a fortnight, until the whole album was available on the site. Have a look and listen to get an idea of the future of the music industry, or just to experience 'Teardrop', the brilliant first single from the album.

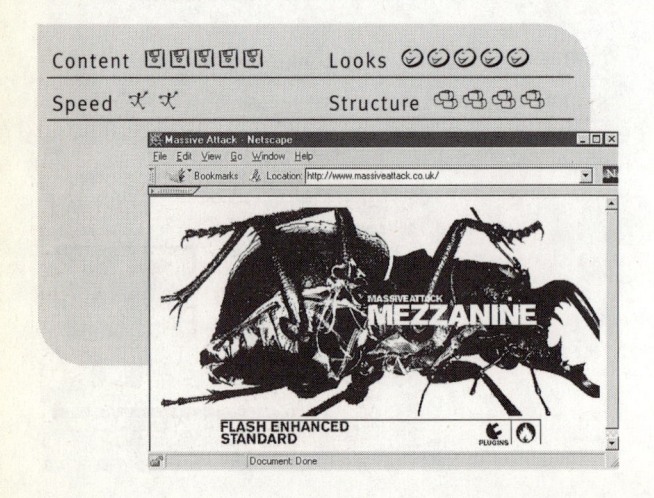

Dance, baby, dance
http://wso.williams.edu/~msly/juke/juke.html

The dancing baby is not new. In fact, after a couple of years of life as a solely Net icon, it has started to take off as a merchandising nightmare. Forget the marketing hype and visit this groovy online jukebox instead. Watch the baby dance to the Beastie Boys' 'Intergalactic', Everything But The Girl's 'Missing', Bob Marley's 'Jammin' or tracks by the Red Hot Chili Peppers, Madonna, Prince, Tori Amos and U2.

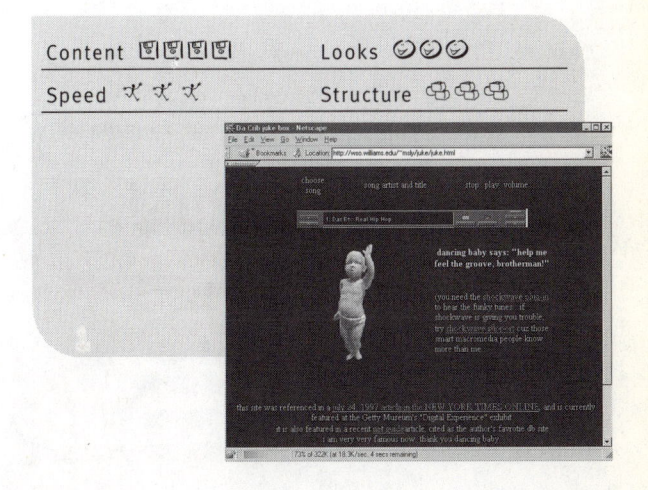

Content	📺📺📺📺	Looks	😊😊😊
Speed	✗ ✗ ✗	Structure	⚘⚘⚘

Music media

http://www.immedia.com.au
http://www.MP3.com

IMMEDIA is a weekly online zine for the Australian music industry. You'll find info on the local scene and the Web music world – like this quote from the creator of MP3 technology, Michael Robertson: 'That tired, old business model that the companies have exploited for decades is not going to work in cyberspace. If the sleeping giants don't open their eyes pretty soon, they are going to lose a huge, multibillion-dollar opportunity to upstarts like me'. Check out his site, too.

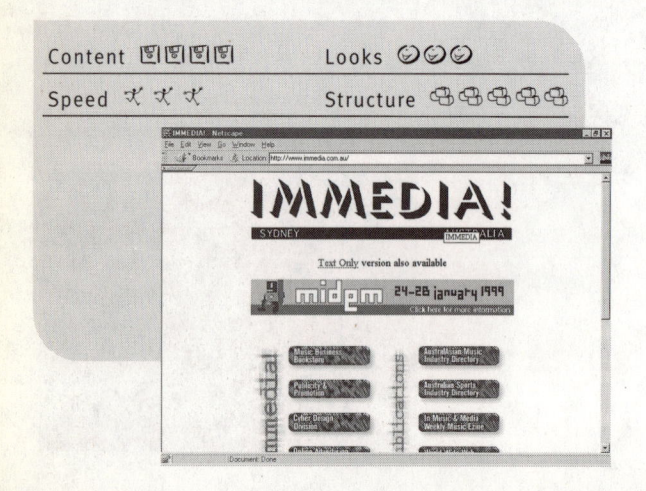

Content 😛😛😛😛   Looks 😊😊😊

Speed ✗ ✗ ✗   Structure 🍥🍥🍥🍥🍥

Listen to the radio
http://www.netradio.net

Get yourself a set of headphones; working in a quiet office will never be the same again. NetRadio's staff of program managers, DJs, writers and editors manage more than 150 constantly updated live audio channels and pre-programmed shows, so you can choose to listen to something new and unexpected each time you tune in, or replay your favourite program. The music content is divided into every category imaginable, from country or Christian hits to classical or jazz to electronica and world music. If you're a 1980s music fan, click on the modern rock link, then select new wave in the pull-down menu.

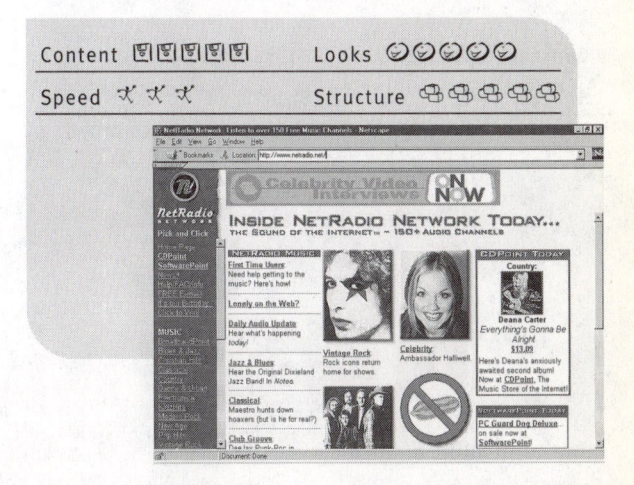

Content 👁👁👁👁👁   Looks 😊😊😊😊😊
Speed ✯✯✯   Structure ♻♻♻♻♻

Music information overload

http://www.imusic.com

You'll have music information coming out of your ears when you reach iMusic. The charts section is mind-blowing. There are full Billboard charts for dance music and country, CD Now sales charts, and iMusic's own listing, showing which artists receive the most interest on its site. The only familiar name in the top ten when I visited was Cher, and the Bee Gees were right up there at number 97. The site also features news, reviews, competitions and live chats.

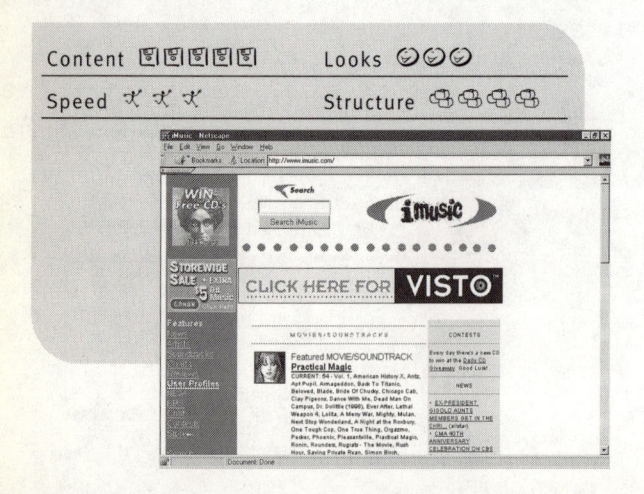

Content 📺📺📺📺
Looks 😊😊😊
Speed ✈✈✈
Structure 💿💿💿💿

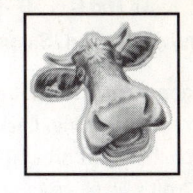

five

Fans and Anti-fans

The Web allows people who feel passionate about something to tell the world about it in their own special way. For some peculiar reason celebrities inspire great passion and Web creativity in others. And in themselves and their promoters too.

Whack Oasis in the face
http://www.urban75.com/Punch/oasis.html

It's about time someone gave these talented thugs a taste of their own medicine. Click your mouse to hit Liam or Noel's face, watch them contort and hear them retaliate with the intelligent 'F*** off'. When you tire of whacking the bad boys of Brit pop, fill in the 'Who I'd really like to smack in the face' form. If you impress the Urban 75 people with your case, they might even add your nomination to the face-punching gallery. Other names on the list include Pauline Hanson, David Beckham, Maggie Thatcher, Rupert Murdoch and whoever created Ally McBeal. Who do you want to smack today?

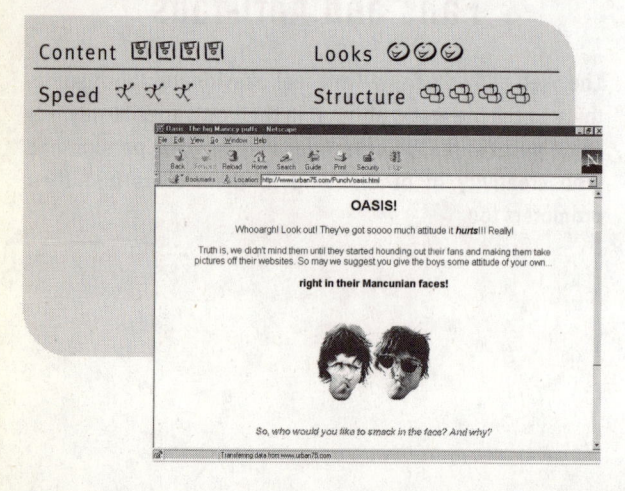

Content 😑😑😑😑	Looks 😊😊😊
Speed ✗ ✗ ✗	Structure 🐸🐸🐸🐸

Throw Bill to the sharks
http://www.bignetwork.com/bz/bg/

What do you do when you spend half a day loading Windows 98 onto your notebook, only to find that your PC brand is the one that clashes with certain bugs in the operating system? Play Throw Bill to the sharks, of course. Punch the little Shockwave version of Gates, who has been topping rich lists again of late, until he falls off the pier. If you prefer, you can save him from the evil hand of death, and hear him say 'I'm not a crook!' It's much more fun to feed him to the circling fins, though. And when you do, you'll find a text message: 'This feeding frenzy best viewed with Internet Explorer 4.0'. Yeah, right.

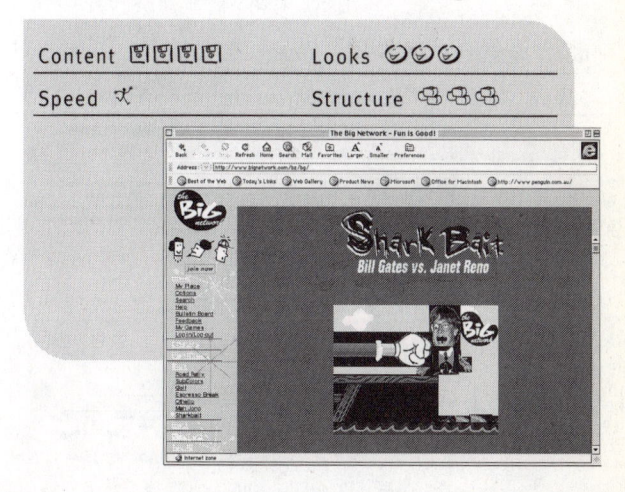

Content 🖾🖾🖾🖾	Looks 😊😊😊
Speed 🕱	Structure 🐚🐚🐚

Do-it-yourself Dannii-bashing
http://apcmag.com/gusworld/dannii/diy.htm

Gusworld has created a super-heroine based on superstar Dannii Minogue: 'By day, she is Dannii Minogue, well-known TV presenter, actress, successful singer and all-round Minogue. When danger threatens, though, she is transformed into Mighty Morphin Dannii Minogue, a mega super-heroine with a strange fondness for tight vinyl costumes and mood lighting.' He's added a story that allows the user to choose its direction: Did she have to a) cancel her latest surgical upgrade; b) buy some extra lip gloss; or c) sorry, I can't tell you what c says. It's rude.

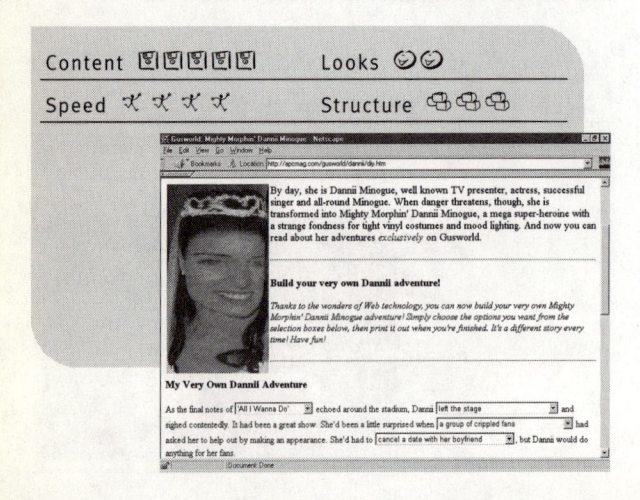

Content 📖📖📖📖📖   Looks 😊😊

Speed ✈✈✈✈   Structure ☁☁☁

Viva whatever

http://apcmag.com/gusworld/music/spice/whatever.htm

Gusworld again: this time it's a Spice Girls site. But why? Gus says: 'Like several million other people around the world, I own both Spice Girls albums (the imaginatively titled *Spice* and *Spiceworld*). I'm not a big enough fan to buy the singles, but I am enough of a music obsessive to want to know what the B-sides, cover versions and other bits of Spice detritus sound like.' So here they are, reviews and links to tracks the girls have recorded or performed, but which are not included on either of their albums. I particularly avoided 'We Are Family' and the live-with-Elton-John version of 'Don't Go Breaking My Heart'.

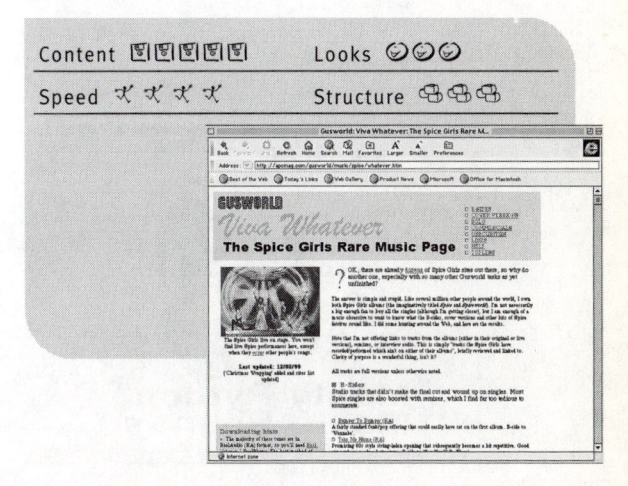

Content	📕📕📕📕	Looks	😊😊😊
Speed	✈✈✈✈	Structure	🔗🔗🔗

Monty Python movie sounds

http://www.starbase21.com/looney/

Remember that great line in *The Holy Grail*: 'We are the knights who say "Ni!"'? What about this classic piece of rally dialogue from *The Life of Brian*: 'You are all individuals!' 'Yes, we are all individuals!'? You'll find yourself in hysterics just reading from the sound-bite lists. After you've listened for long enough, play Barfman. It's a hangman-style game starring the vile Mr Creosote from *The Meaning of Life*. Choose the wrong letter, and he vomits everywhere. If you're wrong too many times, he'll explode. When you guess a word correctly, you get to download a sound clip that matches the word.

Content	Looks
Speed	Structure

The Amazing SPAM Homepage
http://www.cusd.claremont.edu/~mrosenbl/spam.html

Who could argue with 'Ah, Spam, that most inspiring of foods, nectar of the gods, hero of the picnic table'? The Spam Facts section reveals the ham-in-a-can ingredient list, and it's not as bad as you might think: salt, water, sugar, sodium nitrate and chopped pork shoulder meat with added ham meat. According to the Trivia section, 3.8 cans of Spam are consumed each second in the US. Some Spam lovers have also been moved to poetry; see the Spam Fiction section for a taste of this . . .

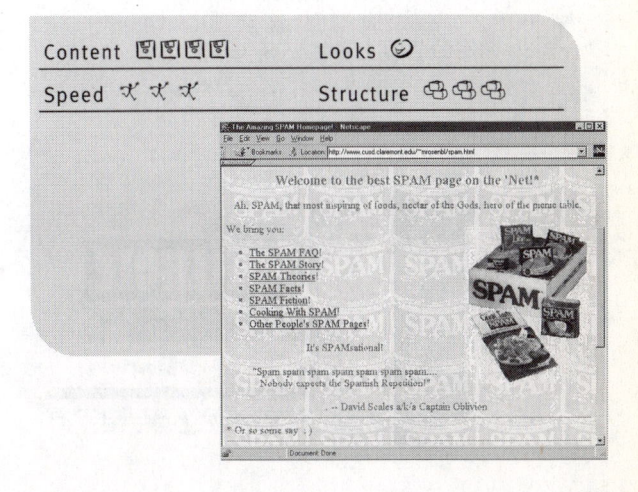

Content 📖📖📖📖	Looks ☺
Speed ✯ ✯ ✯	Structure 🕸🕸🕸

South Park heaven

http://www.thehellhole.com

The Hellhole features images, video clips, transcripts, character profiles and a calendar of episodes. There's a Java chat zone where you can talk about all things *South Park*, a huge fan-mail section, competitions and hundreds of links to other sites. The site is easy to explore and updated every couple of days. Join the mailing list to receive details of site updates and 'secret pages', which are password protected and available only to subscribers. The site was celebrating its four-millionth hit when we visited. That's a lot of *South Park* fans.

Content 🗒🗒🗒🗒🗒 Looks 😊😊

Speed ✡ ✡ Structure 😀😀😀😀

Pride and prejudice
http://www.pemberley.com

Welcome to 'Your haven in a world programmed to misunderstand obsessions with things Austen', as the Republic of Pemberley site describes itself. Join a discussion group on any of the Austen novels or their film adaptations, post your own sequel to or missing scene from an Austen novel, or read up on the author's life and times. If you're a particular fan of the most recent television series of *Pride and Prejudice,* starring Colin Firth and Jennifer Ehle, take a peek at the photo album on **http://orion.it.luc.edu/~avande1/album.html**. The images can be downloaded.

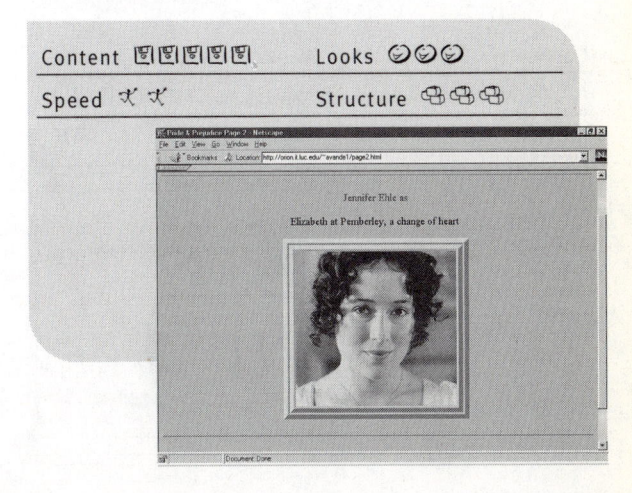

Content	Looks
Speed	Structure

73

Braggtime

http://www.billybragg.co.uk

Billy Bragg's official (they actually prefer not to call it official because that would suggest the involvement of an officious record company, and this site is far too nice for any such involvement to have occurred) Web presence features masterfully executed icons. The little blue house you click on to get home is a particularly pleasing piece of Web art. The site includes the usual discography, tour dates, upcoming releases information, message board and mailing list. The links page is comprehensive, and the non-officious officials encourage the unofficial sites to go forth and multiply.

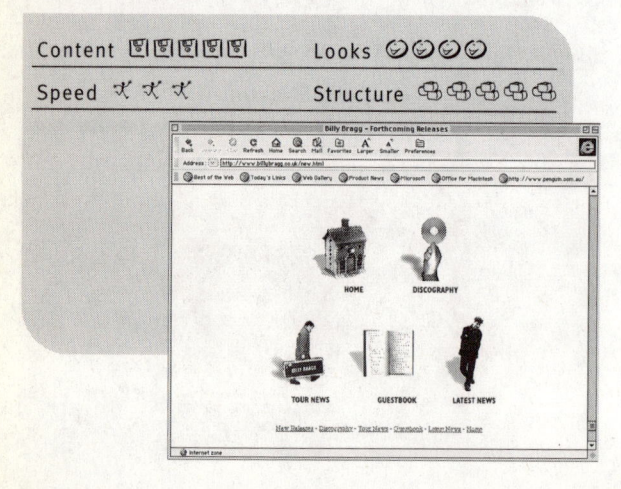

Content 🖫🖫🖫🖫   Looks 😊😊😊😊
Speed ✗ ✗ ✗   Structure 🜲🜲🜲🜲🜲

Keating insults
http://www.webcity.com.au/keating/

The Paul Keating Insults Page is home to great lines like: 'Shut up! Sit down and shut up, you pig!' (to Wilson 'Iron Bar' Tuckey); 'You've been in the dye pot again, Andrew' and 'We're not interested in the views of painted, perfumed gigolos' (to Andrew Peacock); 'Honourable Members opposite squeal like stuck pigs' (on the Coalition in the House of Reps); 'Their existence is putrid. It is absolutely putrid' (on the National Party); and as for his other love, journalists: 'Laurie Oakes [is] a cane toad.' All this, and still Sarah O'Hare couldn't recognise him! If you're a real Paul fan, read his speeches at **www.keating.org.au**.

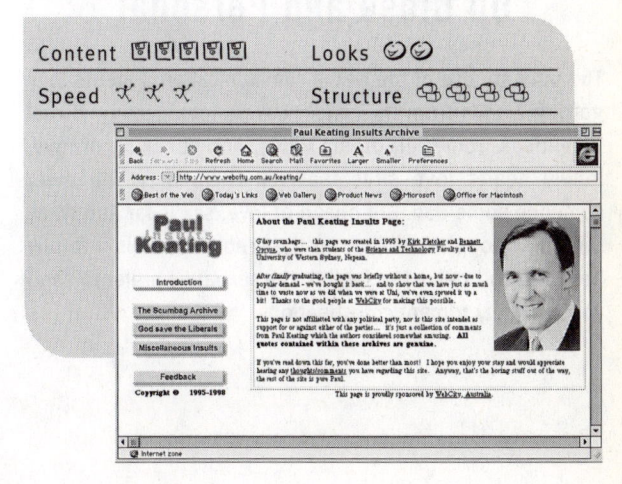

Content Looks
Speed Structure

75

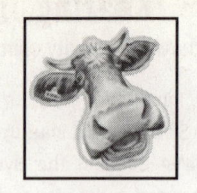

six

Up Close and Personal

The ultimate use of the Net is communication. Parents love getting emails from their kids. Lovers love getting virtual Valentines from their dream dates. And speaking of love, lonely hearts love sites that tell them they will meet someone some day. But ahead of love, sex is far and away the most popular subject on the Web. As this is a family book, I won't delve too far into the sexual – I prefer to send you to purely romantic destinations.

Therapeutic thoughts

http://www.thetherapist.com

You can't get much more personal than opening up to a psychiatrist, though in this case, the therapist isn't real. Nor are his patients. In fact, all the session transcripts you'll read on this site have been invented. 'Depression, schizophrenia, addiction, violence. Sound like your week? No? Welcome to a typical week in the life of Dr Charles Balis.' Balis provides mental health services to Silicon Impressions Inc., a large computer company located in San Francisco. Explore Dr Balis's personal diary and notes, patient diaries and telephone conversations; or travel backstage to create your own characters and therapy sessions.

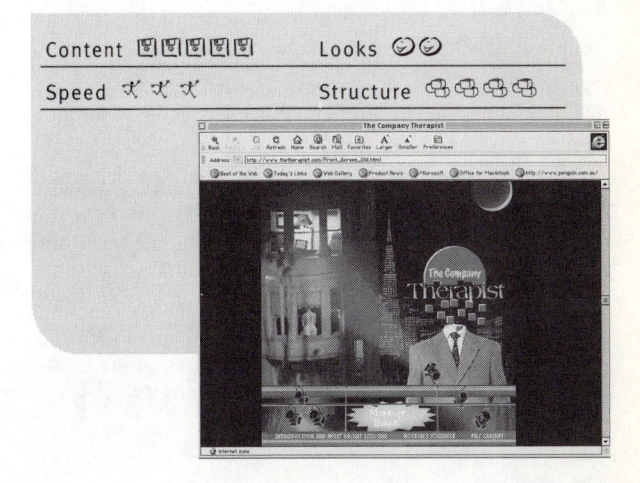

Content 🖥🖥🖥🖥🖥	Looks 😊😊
Speed ✈✈✈	Structure 🐡🐡🐡🐡

Sex and the single Aussie
http://www.durex.com/lounge/au/

On average, Australians have sex 110 times a year, lose their virginity at the age of seventeen, and have 13.1 sexual partners during their lifetime. Twenty-three per cent of us want more, says Durex, the condom manufacturer. Sydney is seen as Australia's sexiest city, ahead of Melbourne and Brisbane, according to the results of the company's annual global survey published on the site. Although this beach-themed site exists to promote Durex products, it also provides useful information on STDs and how to use condoms properly.

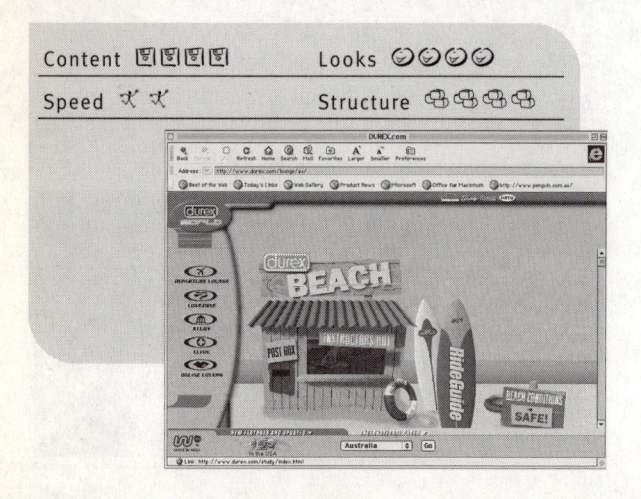

Content 📖📖📖📖	Looks ☺☺☺☺
Speed ✈ ✈	Structure 🐚🐚🐚🐚

Risky questions

http://www.tripod.com/sports/evel/

Evel Knievel, the master of the motorcycle stunt, has switched careers. He's now an online agony aunt. You can ask him about anything you like, from romantic dilemmas to financial crises. Somehow I don't think he'll be able to solve either sort, but his responses are sure to be good for a laugh. The page includes a link to **www.evelknievel.com**, the official Evel site, where you can read useful Knievel facts such as 'Evel will be in Nevada next week and will be participating in the Loughlin Ride with Jay Leno and other celebs. He'll be riding his CMC #1 Evel Knievel Special Model'. Bet you needed to know that.

Content 👎👎👎👎	Looks 😊😊😊
Speed ✗✗✗	Structure ♣♣♣♣

The free cybermarriage site
http://www.geocities.com/Paris/Rue/7130/maina.html

It had to happen. If you can meet and fall in love on the Net, why not tie the virtual knot too? Kanga, the brains behind it all, is a regular on Internet relay chat and ICQ, and wanted to devote a service to the online lovers he saw around him. He's having trouble keeping up with demand — the backlog of marriage hopefuls stood at about 40 at last count. The application form allows for anonymity, and you can choose from several virtual rings, wedding dresses and modes of transport. Scan the pages of weddings gone by for ideas.

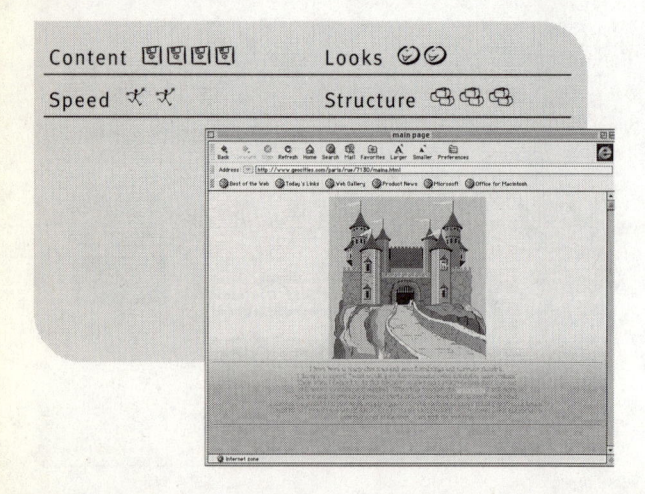

Content 📖📖📖📖	Looks 😊😊
Speed ✈✈	Structure 🌐🌐🌐

I had sex with Clinton
http://www.ihadsexwithclinton.com

Sisters of Monica unite! This is the place where you bravely confess to your Clinton affair by filling in the blanks provided: 'At Bill's second inaugural ball in 1996, he approached me in front of a large, swan-shaped punch bowl. After describing my chest as "world class", he went on to describe my lips as "more appealing than Boris Yeltsin's" and invited me for a quick limo ride to show me the "real Washington monument".' Then you send it off, and hope the team behind the site finds it amusing enough to send you your own 'I had sex with Bill Clinton' T-shirt.

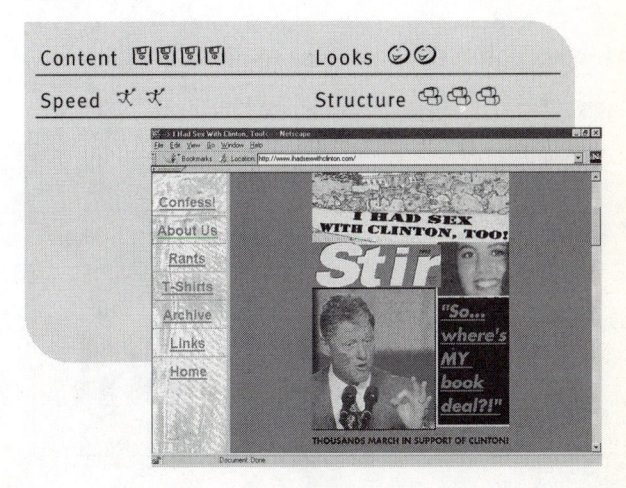

Content	📖📖📖📖	Looks	😊😊
Speed	✈✈	Structure	🔗🔗🔗

Virtual chocolates
http://www.virtualchocolate.com/mothersday/

If you're one of those people who think Mother's Day is a retail industry plot to sell more flowers and chocolates, a virtual Mother's Day card may be the answer come May. The cards are free and won't give the most important woman in your life hay fever or weight problems. Unfortunately, the images are enough to send you down the street to buy yourself a box of chocolates.

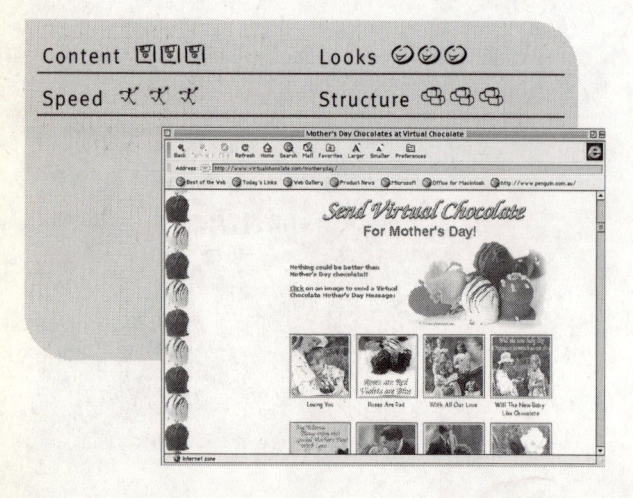

Content 🖻🖻🖻	Looks 😊😊😊
Speed ✼ ✼ ✼	Structure 🍩🍩🍩

Father, dear Father's Day
http://www.aristotle.net/fathersday/

Send dad a virtual Father's Day card in September. This site is the slickest Dad's Day offering online, although because it's American it thinks Father's Day is in June. But the graphics are groovy and, besides cards, there's a section where you can post a tribute to your father and read what others have written. There's also a selection of, um, fatherly links and a trivia game.

Content ▣▣▣▣▣   Looks ☺☺☺☺

Speed ✄ ✄ ✄   Structure ♧♧♧♧

Life calculator
http://www.hksrch.com.hk/life.html

If you're an exercise-mad teetotaller, this site will make you very happy. It's a questionnaire that estimates the duration of your life based on age, health, gender, lifestyle and family history. The good news is, if you get to the end of the quiz and know you're not looking good, you can click on the 'Forget it!' button rather than proceed to collect your estimate. You can also run the whole thing in Chinese – the site is run by Timmy Yu, a Hong Kong-based psychology student.

Content 📺📺📺📺	Looks 😊
Speed ✈ ✈	Structure 🐠🐠🐠🐠

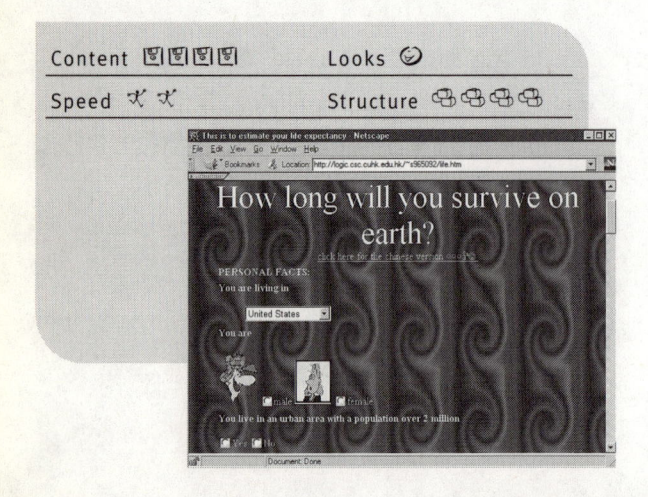

Love calculator
http://www.lovecalculator.com

Remember those games played at school with pens, paper and hopeless lovesick dreams? The ones where you wrote down a girl's name, a boy's name, counted the number of letters in common, then added the other letters together in an entirely nonsensical manner until you got an answer? Well, in these new-fangled times, you don't need the paper or even the maths. Type the names in, cry when your score is below average, then remember it's even sillier and less relevant to real life and love than an astrological report in a weekly women's magazine.

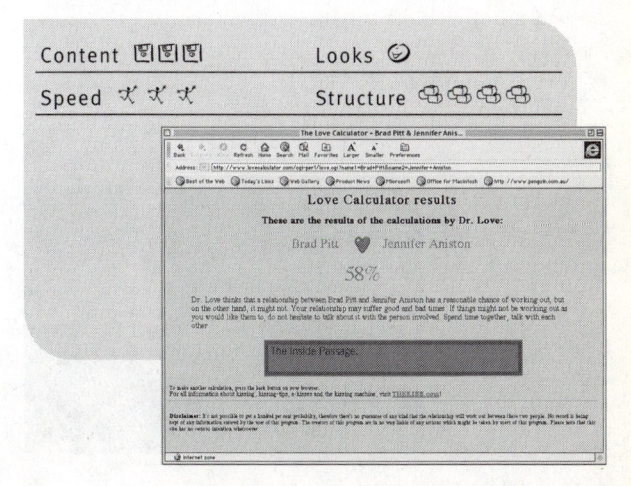

Content	📖📖📖	Looks	☺
Speed	✈ ✈ ✈	Structure	🏠🏠🏠🏠

Astrosurfology
http://www.jessicaadams.com.au/astrology

Speaking of astrology, which we of course do not believe in for one moment but love to read to each other over coffee, meet Jessica Adams, the Australian Web authority. She's also big in magazines, books (*Single White E-mail* is her first work of fiction) and newspapers, but that's by the by. Find out about your five personal planets – Sun, Moon, Mercury, Venus and Mars – by visiting 'You are five people trapped in one body'.

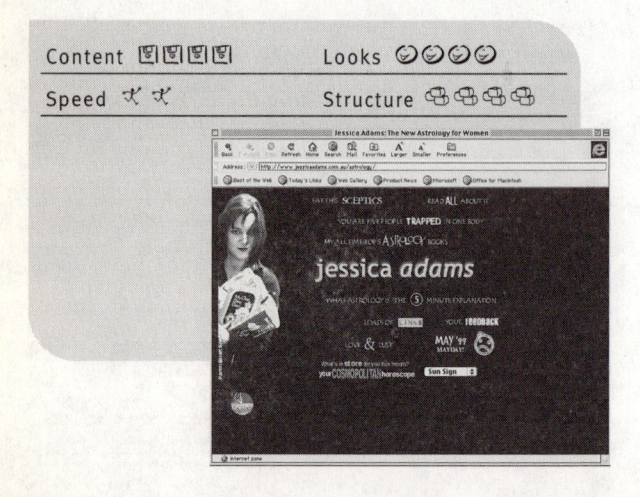

Content 📖📖📖📖	Looks ☺☺☺☺
Speed ✗ ✗	Structure 🐢🐢🐢🐢

Love quotes
http://www.from.aus.com/love/

All you need is love – John Lennon
At the touch of love, everyone becomes a poet – Plato
To love is not to look at one another, but to look together in the same direction – Antoine de Saint-Exupéry
The heart was made to be broken – Oscar Wilde

Finding it hard to express your feelings for someone? Drop in here and steal some other brilliant thinker's romantic words, or just spend some time philosophising about love.

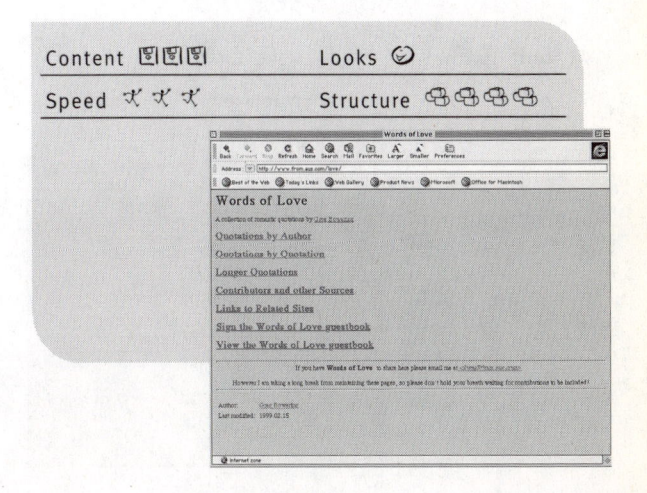

Content	📖📖📖	Looks	☺
Speed	✈✈✈	Structure	⊛⊛⊛⊛

Going to the chapel

http://www.wednet.com

Wednet describes itself as the Internet's premier wedding planning site. It's filled with useful pieces of advice for brides-to-be, such as this one on garters: 'Buy two – one to keep and one to throw!'. You'll find everything you need to know about making your own veil, whether you should serve alcohol at the reception (they have to be kidding, right?), whether kids should be included in the day's festivities (depends on the kids), and the alternatives to diamonds for engagement rings. The Frequently Asked Questions section covers everything from concealing tattoos to honouring a deceased spouse.

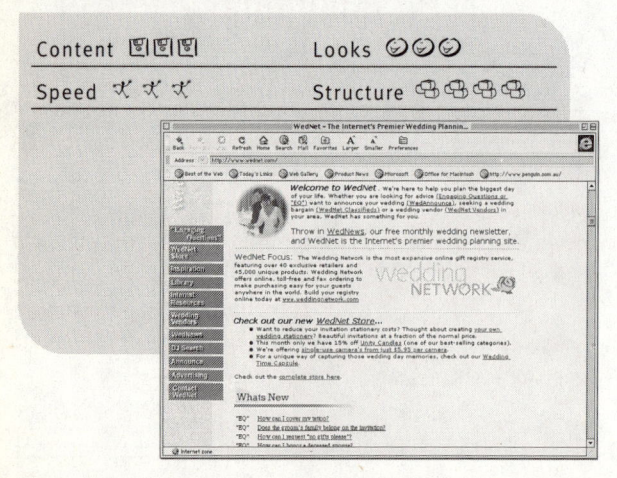

Content 📖📖📖	Looks 😊😊😊
Speed ✈ ✈ ✈	Structure 🍀🍀🍀🍀

seven

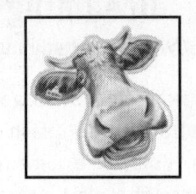

Shopping

Busy people love shopping online. It's handy, too, for sending gifts to friends and families overseas. Why buy a book here and post it to the US when you can order it to be delivered direct through Amazon.com? Browsing through online shopping sites can save you time and help you pin down exactly what you're looking for before you go out to real stores. It's best suited to buying the kinds of staples you can order without trying them on, such as wine, theatre tickets and roses (not so good for tailored suits). No more queuing when you shop on the Net.

Dreaming of Dinnigan

http://www.collettedinnigan.com.au

The rich colours and gorgeous fabrics that combine to form Collette Dinnigan's fashions translate surprisingly well to the Web. It may take some time to download the full-sized photographs of her most recent collection on the catwalk, but if you're serious about looking for a seriously expensive but special dress, you'll wait. To order a Dinnigan creation, click on the global stockists link, then on the Australian section of the world map that appears. Dinnigan is just one of many great Australian designers now promoting their work online. Search for your other favourites, from Zimmerman to Morrissey to Trent Nathan.

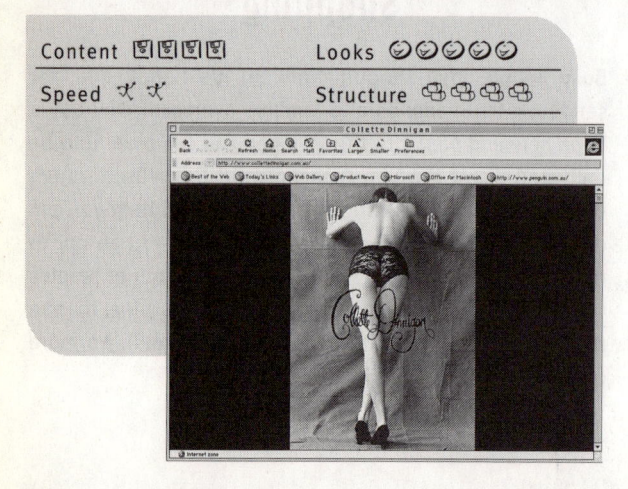

Content	🖻🖻🖻🖻	Looks	😊😊😊😊😊
Speed	✈✈	Structure	🏵🏵🏵🏵

Feral Cheryl

http://www.feralcheryl.com.au

Australia's answer to Barbie, Feral Cheryl was born on the northern coast of NSW, which explains her dreadlocks, bare feet, naturally brown hair, tattoos, simple clothes, healthy body shape and bag of dried herbs (herbs!). Her creators have been pleased with the media attention she has received, if a little confused at the response to Cheryl's pubic hair. We all have it from a certain age, after all. She arrives with a poster explaining her non-consumer lifestyle; no other accessories are available. The site includes a link to a Real Audio Feral Cheryl theme song by North Coast band Bentmettle.

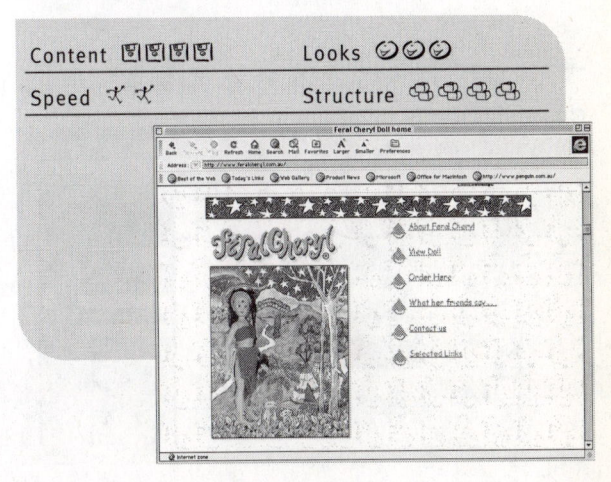

Content	🔲🔲🔲🔲	Looks	☺☺☺
Speed	✄ ✄	Structure	🐚🐚🐚🐚

Bag yourself a boat
http://www.charterguide.com.au

The Australian Charter Guide's web site lists thousands of boats for hire according to name, company name, desired area and activity, type of boat and capacity. Read a couple of articles about boats and expeditions, enter the odd competition to win a cruise, or plan your own fishing, diving or sailing trip.

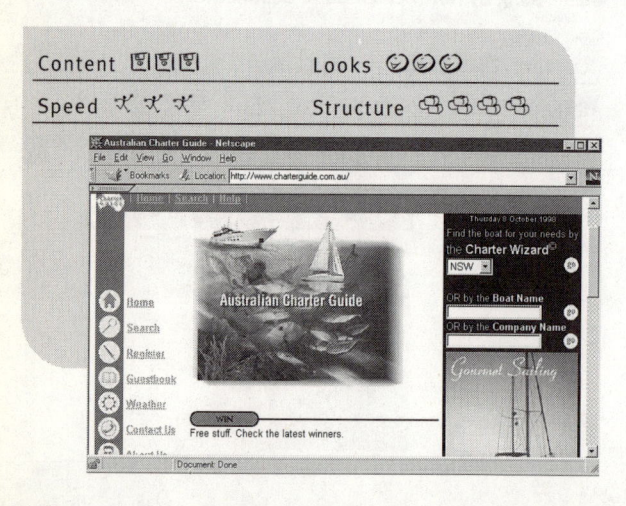

Content 📖📖📖 Looks 😊😊😊
Speed ✗ ✗ ✗ Structure 🐢🐢🐢🐢

Video is easy

http://www.reel.com

Reel.com hires and sells a vast selection of video tapes and disks (although Australians can only buy). The 85 000 movies available vary in price and format, from $US4.99 to $US17.99. The database is searchable by genre, title, actor or director. During 1998 the owners of mega-retailer Hollywood Video paid about $US100 million for a piece of Reel's e-commerce action.

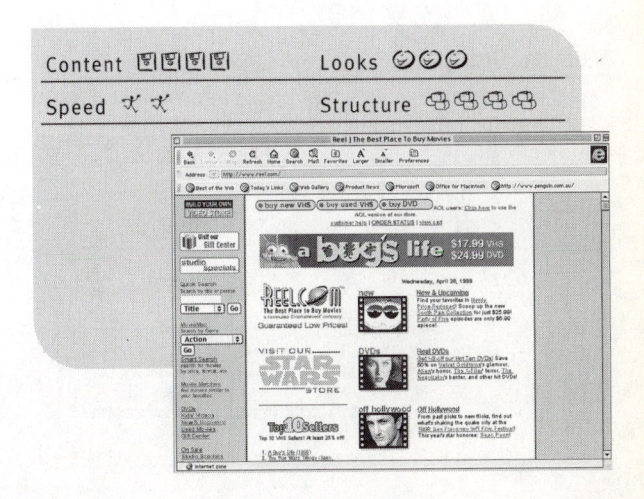

Content 📖📖📖📖	Looks ☺☺☺
Speed ✈✈	Structure 🖴🖴🖴🖴

Select a dog breed

http://www.petnet.com.au/dogselectapet.html

Fill in the questionnaire and Selectapet will help you choose your next dog. 'Choosing the correct type of dog can be difficult. Should it be large or small, active or gentle, hairy or smooth coated?' It's a bit like choosing a partner, isn't it? Once you've answered the questions, PetNet will suggest a few breeds that would be suitable for you and your lifestyle. The rest of the site is a terrific resource for pet owners.

Content 📖📖📖	Looks 😊😊
Speed 🏃🏃🏃	Structure 🏗🏗🏗

Sporting goods
http://www.rebelsport.com.au

Rebel Sport now sells stuff like tennis racquets, running shoes and swimsuits from its web site. Check out the running-shoe selection guide or ski-hire section, or send in your sporting club or association's details to get a free Web presence. This site should really appear in the sport section of the book as well. Its links section, 'Your Sport', is comprehensive and easy to use.

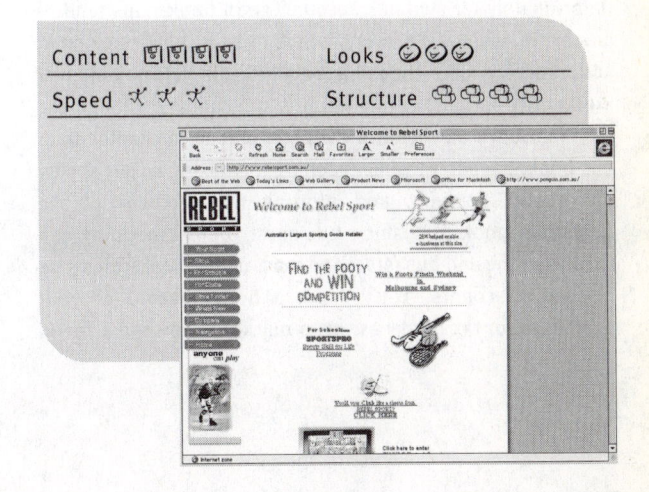

Content	📖📖📖	Looks	😊😊😊
Speed	✗ ✗ ✗	Structure	🔗🔗🔗🔗

Bookshopping

http://www.amazon.com
http://bookshop.blackwell.co.uk
http://www.codysbooks.com
http://www.gleebooks.com.au
http://www.thewell.com.au
http://www.dymocks.com.au
http://www.coop-bookshop.com.au
http://www.readings.com.au
http:// www.ariel.com.au
http://www.shearersbookshop.com.au

Unfortunately for my bank account, good bookshops tend to lure me in, with intent, every couple of days. I love looking at and touching and choosing between the latest works of literary fiction on the front counter or scanning through the Internet books up the back (OK, so I belong in chapter 14 of this book, I admit it), while listening to relaxing music, spying on fellow shoppers, and plotting my takeover of the Australian book publishing business. Online shopping can save you time and bus fares, and most online bookstores give massive discounts. You'll have a better record of your purchases for tax purposes. It's a quick way to send a friend in the US or UK a present. You can order books that haven't made it into local bookstores, read reviews, discover books of similar ilk to the one you're after and find out details of upcoming online and in-store events at a bookshop near you. Eventually, of course, you'll be able to download novels to groovy little electronic book viewers, like the Rocket eBook (check out **www.nuvomedia.com** for more).

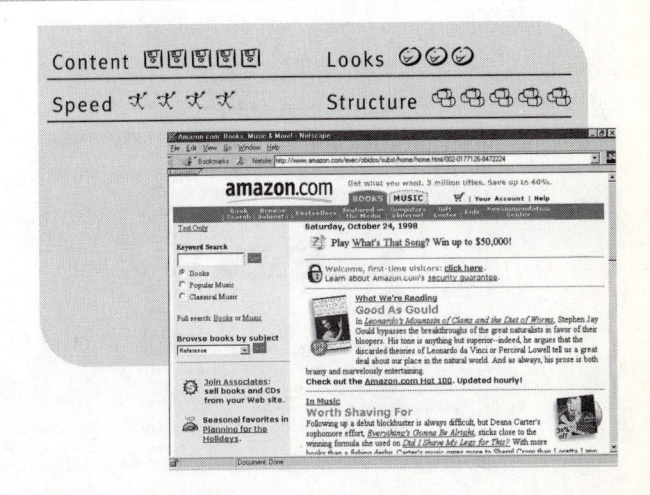

Content 😒😒😒😒 Looks 😊😊😊

Speed ✗ ✗ ✗ ✗ Structure 🐚🐚🐚🐚🐚

Recorded music online

http://www.cmm.com.au
http://www.cdnow.com

CD vouchers make the perfect gift for someone who loves music. Now you can pay for them online (securely by credit card) and send them to friends or family by email (personal message included). Australia's Chaos Music Market also allows visitors to download CD-quality singles over the Net via a technology called Liquid Audio. CMM sells music in every format you can imagine, from vinyl to DVD. CD Now, the Amazon of the music industry, even lets you compile your own CD for purchase (although the choice of tracks may be limited).

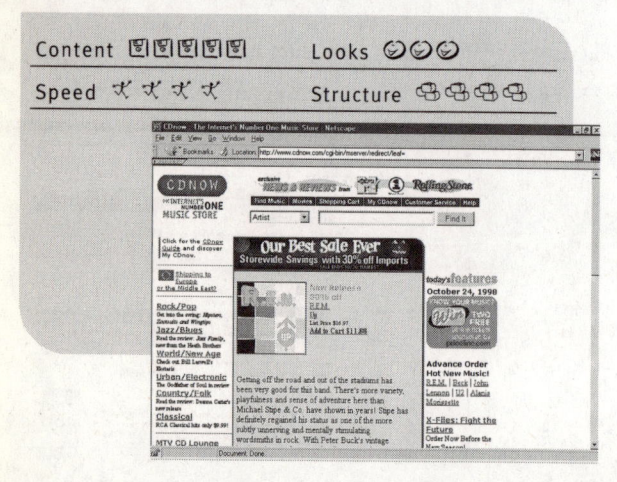

Content 🎵🎵🎵🎵🎵   Looks ☺☺☺
Speed ✗ ✗ ✗ ✗   Structure 🐛🐛🐛🐛

Tickets without the queue

http://www.ticketek.com.au

This must be one of the most useful sites in the country. Ticketek online provides a program of upcoming events, price and availability details, and reviews. But most importantly, it allows you to buy your tickets online without queuing or waiting to get through on the phone. Worried about putting your credit-card details up for the world to hack? The tech-heads say files are encrypted at the customer's end and decrypted at Ticketek's end with Ticketek's private encryption key, so there is less risk of credit-card fraud than when paying over the phone or at a point-of-sale terminal.

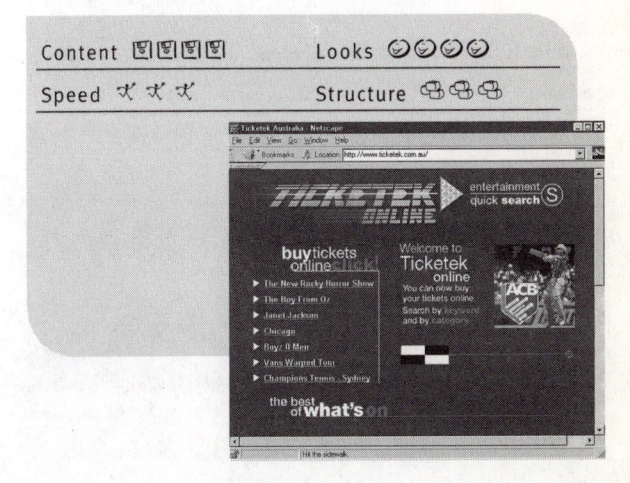

Content 🖳🖳🖳	Looks 😊😊😊😊
Speed ✗ ✗ ✗	Structure 🐛🐛🐛

Real and virtual flowers
http://www.interflora.com.au

Send someone flowers today. The Interflora web site lets you order real flowers and send them just about anywhere in the world. It's *so* much better than doing it by phone, because you can see what the flowers look like, and I reckon they look good. If you can't afford the real thing, choose from a selection of virtual bouquets. There are plenty of free e-flowers to choose from.

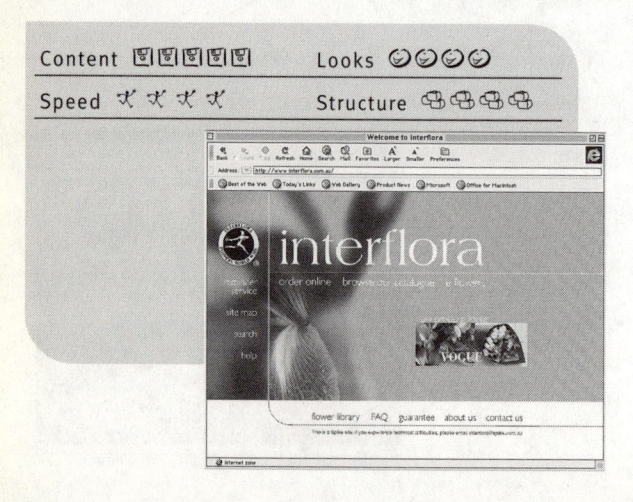

Content	📖📖📖📖	Looks	☺☺☺☺
Speed	✗ ✗ ✗ ✗	Structure	🌐🌐🌐🌐

Online grog
http://www.liquorlink.com.au

Forget about lugging heavy boxes filled with wine that might pass the taste test home from the bottle shop. Order your booze online through Liquorlink. They guarantee satisfaction: 'If you taste a bottle of wine and you are dissatisfied, we will collect the remainder of that wine at our expense and credit your account with the full price.' One of the great things about online retailers is that they up their level of service to compete with the real-world operators. In Liquorlink's case, this means quaffers can make use of a special-occasions email quote service, wine tips and an email newsletter.

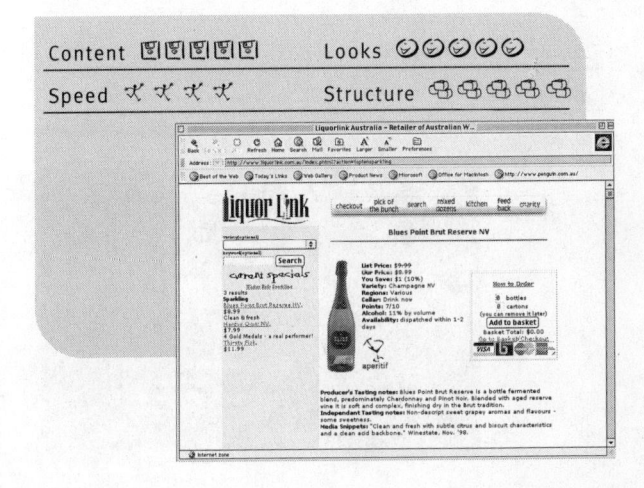

Content	😑😑😑😑	Looks	😊😊😊😊😊
Speed	✗ ✗ ✗ ✗	Structure	🐚🐚🐚🐚🐚

Gadget heaven

http://www.sharperimage.com

Chapel Street in South Yarra is home to a real Sharper Image store, so Melburnians may be familiar with the home of super-gadgets. The online version is American, but the gadgets are great. If you're after a Mini Scooter Rollerboard, Multi-Tool & Pocketknife Collection, Turbo Digital Tie Rack (every home should have one), a Soft Sound Hairdryer or some similarly unusual gift for the friend who has everything, this site should be high on your list of Web destinations.

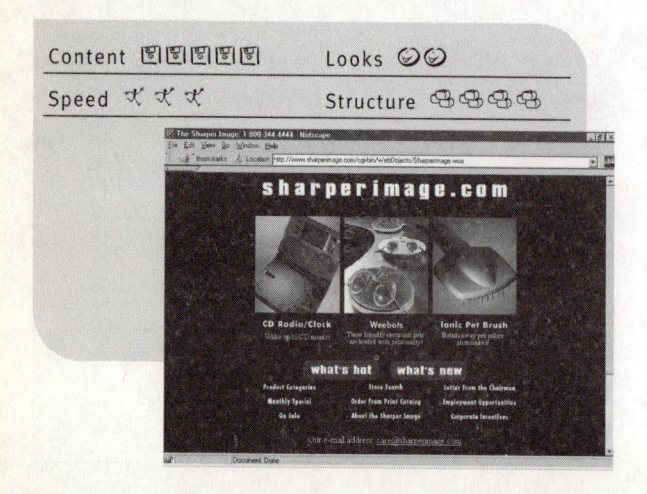

Content	👎👎👎👎	Looks	☺☺
Speed	✗ ✗ ✗	Structure	🐸🐸🐸🐸

Market fresh
http://www.greengrocer.com.au

This is a Web fruit and vegetable specialist for those who live in the Sydney metropolitan area, the Blue Mountains, Wollongong and the NSW Central Coast – and soon, Perth, Melbourne and Brisbane as well. For NSW residents, **greengrocer.com** delivers fresh produce from Sydney's Flemington markets straight to your home, and also lets you keep tabs on your shopping habits. Greengrocer gift vouchers are available.

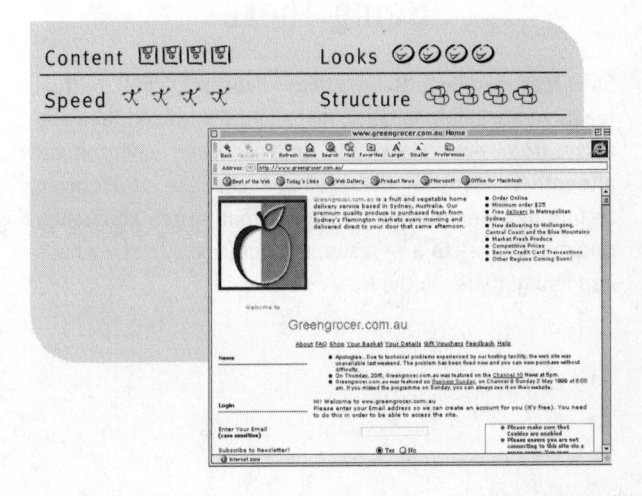

Content	🗒🗒🗒🗒	Looks	😊😊😊😊
Speed	✮ ✮ ✮ ✮	Structure	🏵🏵🏵🏵

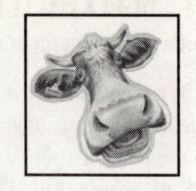

eight

Being There

Sites featuring beautiful graphics, Webcams, VRML (virtual reality modelling language), maps and diaries can take you away from your desk and into another environment altogether. Many of these sites make use of Webcam technology – employing a camera that sends constantly updated images to a web site, allowing users to see what's happening there via the Net.

World Webcams
http://www.steveweb.com/80clicks/

Don't be put off by the slightly dorky tagline: 'Around the World in 80 Clicks', or by the little balloon-and-globe animated gif. This site may not look cool, but it provides links to Webcams that beam views of Montreal, New York, Paris, Helsinki, Karachi, Jerusalem, Venice (California, not Italy, but both are lovely) and more than 70 other cities to your PC. Explore the 'About' section to find links to other mega Webcam sites.

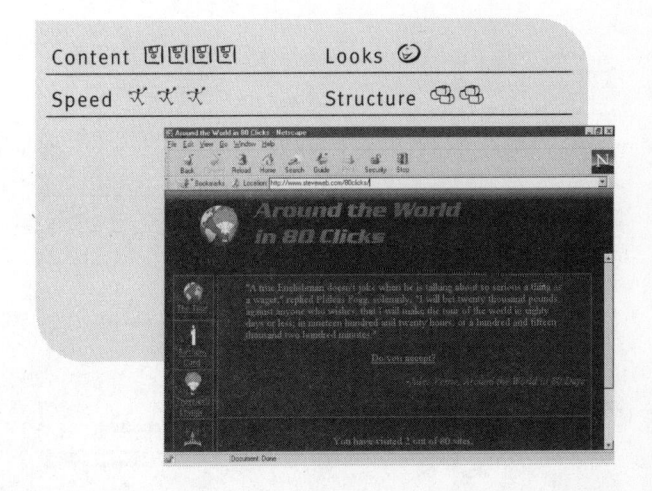

Content 画画画画	Looks ☺
Speed ✗ ✗ ✗	Structure ♋♋

City guides

http://www.citysearch.com.au
http://www.sidewalk.com.au

Want to see a movie, but can't find the paper to see what's on? Hungry, but not sure which restaurants in your area serve decent vegetarian meals? Wondering what time the footy kicks off on Saturday or what time the art gallery closes this afternoon? Try your local city guide. Two of the biggest American city-guide operators have set up shop in Australia: Citysearch, a joint venture here with Fairfax; and Sidewalk, the Microsoft offering, which you'll find through Ninemsn.

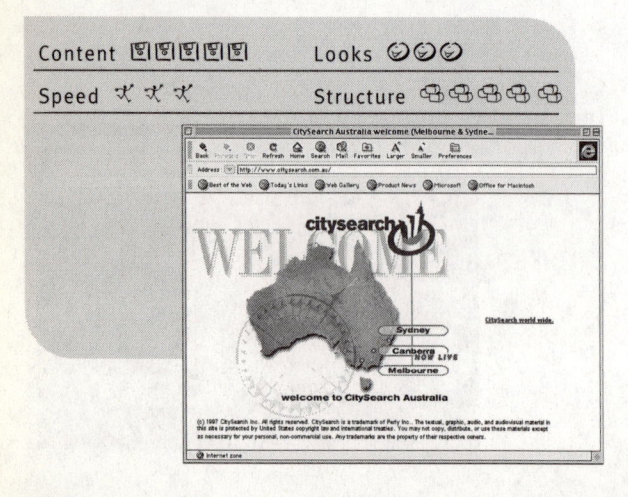

Content 📖📖📖📖📖　　Looks 😊😊😊

Speed ✰✰✰　　　　　Structure 🐢🐢🐢🐢🐢

Streets of London

http://uk.multimap.com

Homesick Poms with map fetishes and Australians planning trips to the UK will find this interactive map site respectively nostalgia-inspiring and useful. Click anywhere on the map of Britain to zoom in for a closer look, or type in the name of a city, town, postcode or London street for a detailed view. You can then click to see the same-sized view one tile to the east, north, west or south too. Print out the pages you need, and forget about buying a street directory.

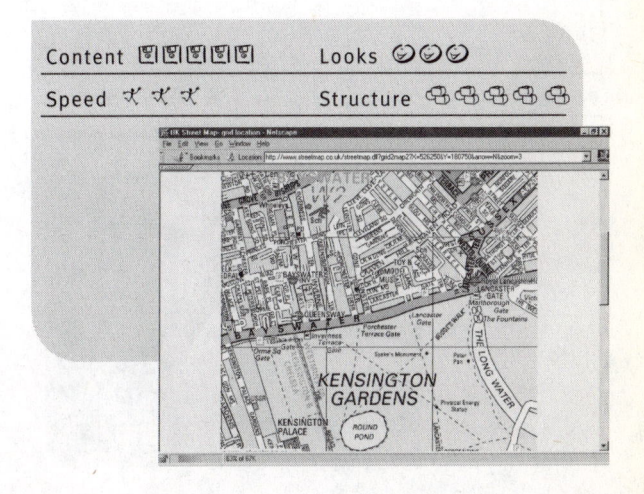

Content 📖📖📖📖   Looks 😊😊😊
Speed ✈✈✈   Structure 🕸🕸🕸🕸🕸

White sails in the sunset

http://www.soh.nsw.gov.au

The Opera House was officially opened by Queen Elizabeth II on 20 October 1973, so it celebrated its 25th birthday during 1998. The web site that appeared as part of the party features a history of the Australian icon, menus of its restaurants, event and tour information and booking details. Mouseover the Opera House symbol on the index page to see a stunning array of photos, including one that looks as though it was taken at the incredible final Crowded House concert held there.

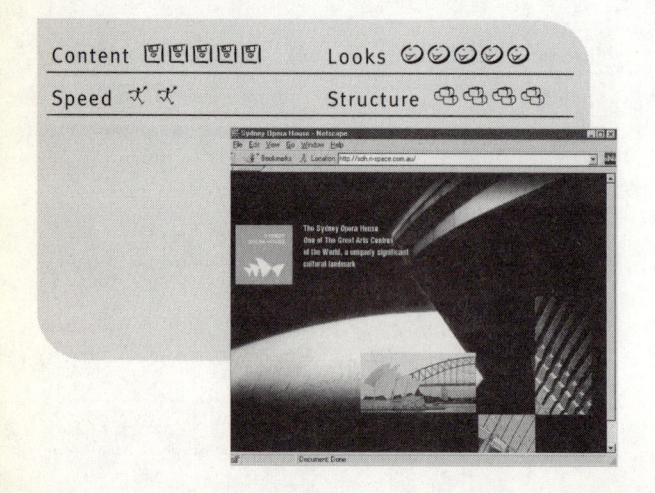

Content 📄📄📄📄 Looks 😊😊😊😊😊

Speed ✈ ✈ Structure 🌐🌐🌐🌐

Hip and groovy art
http://www.mca.com.au

Take a look around a current or past exhibition. In the archived section of this very groovy site (hey, it's the Museum of Contemporary Art in Sydney, and you can't get much hipper than that), you'll find a link to the Keith Haring exhibition, which was moving and impressive when it appeared in reality at the Circular Quay museum back in 1996. The works stand up well online. Multimedia elements include audio, video and animated gif versions of some of Haring's creations. Elsewhere at the MCA online, keep track of events and merchandise, find out how to join, or follow the cool links page to more art online.

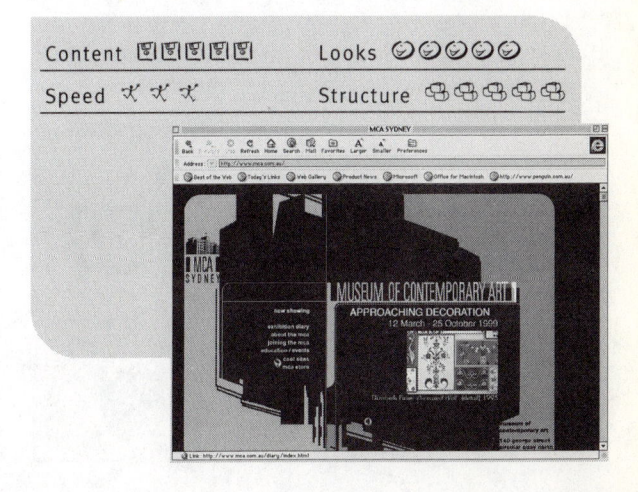

Content ▣▣▣▣▣   Looks ☺☺☺☺☺
Speed ✄✄✄   Structure ♻♻♻♻♻

Long macchiato

http://www.altespresso.com.au

Wander into this online café and you'll feel as though you're in a hip café in Sydney's Surry Hills – which you are, in a virtual sense. Flick through the newspapers and zines, browse the latest arts and film links, and make yourself at home. This site also features the Altcam Webcam of the physical café and its customers, refreshed every two minutes (the café, not the customers) between 7 a.m. and 10 p.m. You can also make yourself a virtual cappuccino by clicking on the right bits of the machine and placing the cup and milk jug in the right spots at the right time. The sound effects are spot on, too.

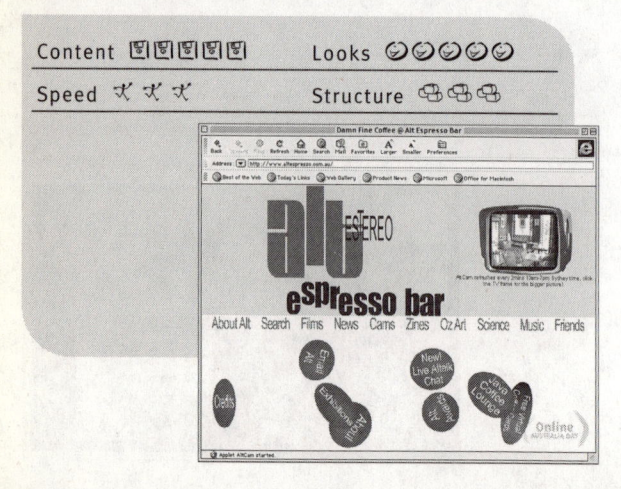

Content 🖺🖺🖺🖺🖺	Looks 😊😊😊😊😊
Speed ✈ ✈ ✈	Structure 🐌🐌🐌

Marvellous Mardi Gras
http://www.mardigras.com.au

Well, 750 000 partying spectators can't be wrong. The Sydney Gay & Lesbian Mardi Gras Parade is an all-singing, all-dancing entertainment extravaganza, held around the beginning of March each year. Find out more about what the event means to the world's gays and lesbians now, and what it meant to its pioneers 20 or so years ago when it was first held. In 1998 and 1999, a Webcast unit beamed the two-hour event live to the world. Let's hope they return every year. The site is also home to Sleaze Ball (October) information.

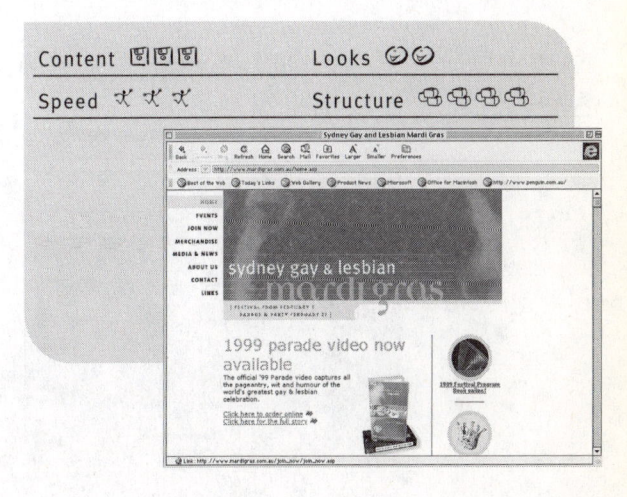

Content 📄📄📄   Looks 😊😊
Speed ✈✈✈   Structure 🌀🌀🌀🌀

Lest we forget
http://www.awm.gov.au

Museums translate well to the Web because of the terrific archiving facility. The Australian War Memorial's national collections database includes film, sound, official and private records and the Roll of Honour. If you can't make it to Canberra on Anzac Day, try visiting the web site one year instead. It has a page dedicated to the anniversary of the first major military action by Australian and New Zealand forces during World War I, on 25 April 1915, the day the Allied expedition landed at Gallipoli. It's beautifully written and illustrated.

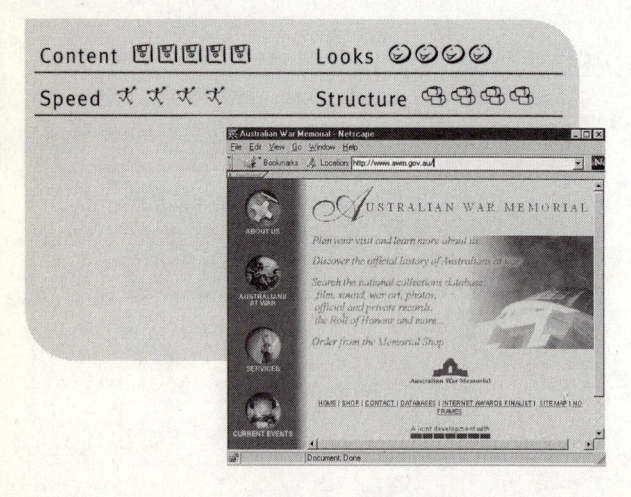

Content	📖📖📖📖	Looks	☺☺☺☺
Speed	✈✈✈✈	Structure	🌐🌐🌐🌐

Discover the world
http://www.discovery.com

The Discovery Channel's web site is brilliant! Discovery News Brief covers world science news; Earth Alert provides daily natural-disaster updates, and Orangutan and Shark Cams take you to the zoo online. Watch an orangutan hang around at the National Zoo in Washington DC, or a shark swimming around the Waikiki Aquarium from the comfort – and safety – of your PC.

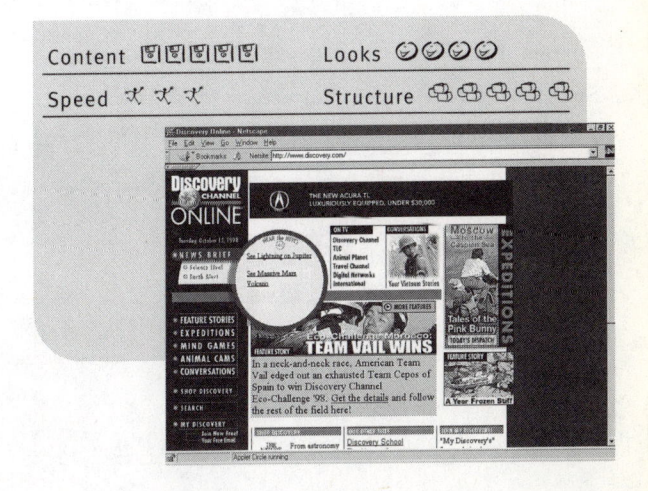

Content 📖📖📖📖📖	Looks 😊😊😊😊
Speed ✈✈✈	Structure 🐢🐢🐢🐢🐢

Ingrid on ice
http://www.abc.net.au/science/antarctica/ingrid/

Ingrid McGauchey was the doctor at Mawson Station, Antarctica, during 1998. Read her Web diary of the year, which is archived on the ABC site, and find out why she decided to go work with other people who were freezing their socks off, how cold it really was, and what it's like to live in such isolation from the rest of the world. She posted some gorgeous polar images during the time she was there, too.

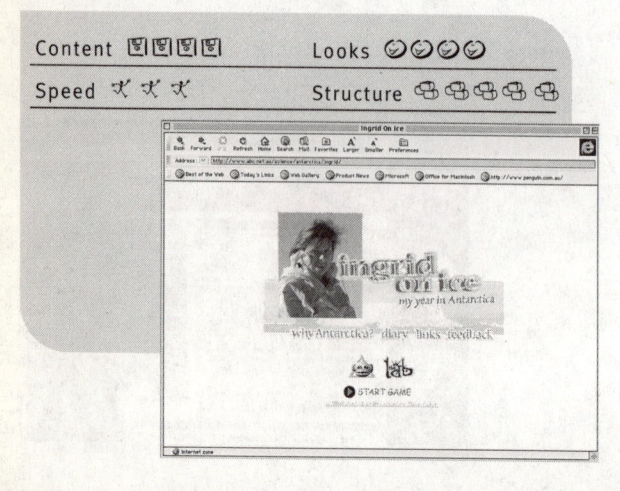

Content 📖📖📖📖 Looks 😊😊😊😊
Speed 🏃 🏃 🏃   Structure 🐢🐢🐢🐢🐢

Homesick Australians abroad

http://www.coolabah.com/oz/

A browse through the message board on this site will remind you of all the things you'd miss if you lived overseas. The most common request is for information about the footy. The Events section goes one better, and even provides training times for the New York Australian Rules Football Club in Central Park. Kate Juliff, an Australian living in Manhattan, set up the site with fellow New Yorker Richard Rankin to provide feature articles and resources for Australians living abroad. The site includes links to Australian media and government sites and articles that give an insight into the expat lifestyle.

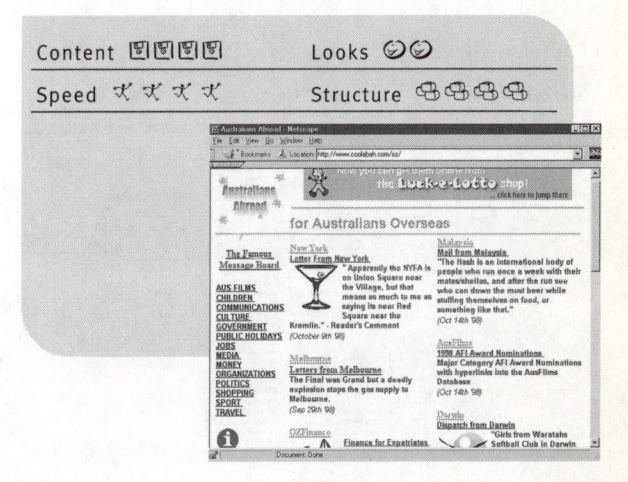

Content	📖📖📖📖	Looks	😊😊
Speed	✗ ✗ ✗ ✗	Structure	⊕⊕⊕⊕

2000 or bust
http://www.everything2000.com

The bright-yellow theme running through this site reminds you of the fluoro reflector strips on kids' bicycle helmets, but the site's developers needn't have gone to such lengths to get our attention. This place is home to bucketloads of news and information about the millennium, from how to save the world by debugging your PC, to where to celebrate on New Year's Eve.

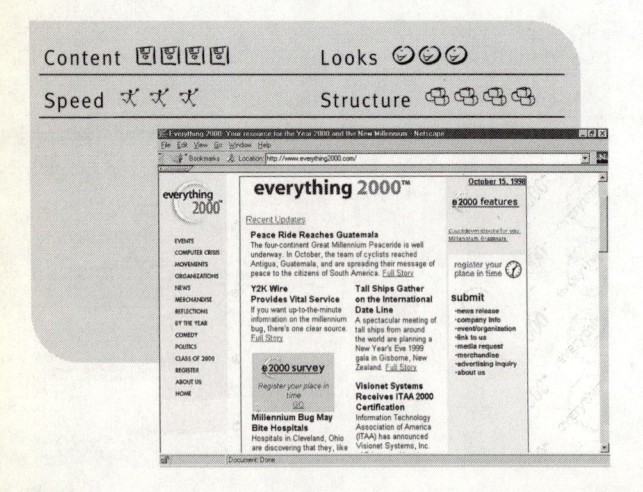

Content	📖📖📖📖	Looks	☺☺☺
Speed	✈✈✈	Structure	♧♧♧♧

Florentines
http://english.firenze.net/qtvr/

QTVR (QuickTime Virtual Reality) is a technology that allows you to scroll around an image so that you can view it from all angles. Florence, being a city of art and architecture, was made for this, so this site is one that art-lovers and armchair travellers alike should not miss. The Ponte Vecchio and Arno view is stunning in virtual reality. (The food and people of Italy, on the other hand, must be experienced first hand.) This site also provides Citysearch-style information about Florence and links to Webcams and maps.

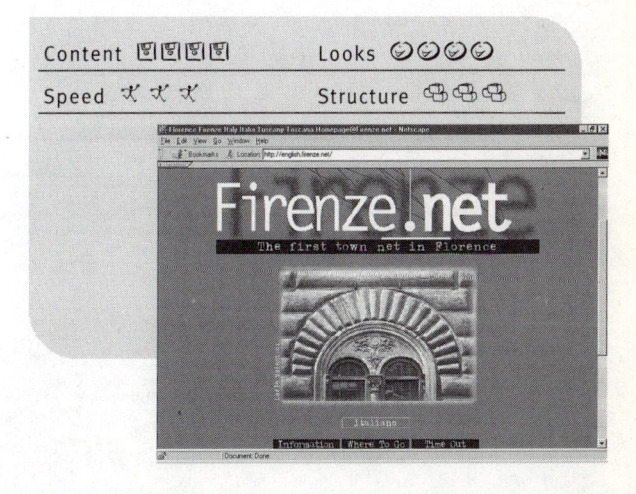

Content	📖📖📖📖	Looks	☺☺☺☺
Speed	✈✈✈	Structure	⌘⌘⌘

View from a robotic telescope

http://www.telescope.org/rti/

The 46-centimetre Bradford Robotic Telescope lives in West Yorkshire, England, but you can access it through the Web. It decides when conditions are good enough to look at the northern sky, and prioritises the Web requests, scheduling viewing time accordingly. No astronomers necessary.

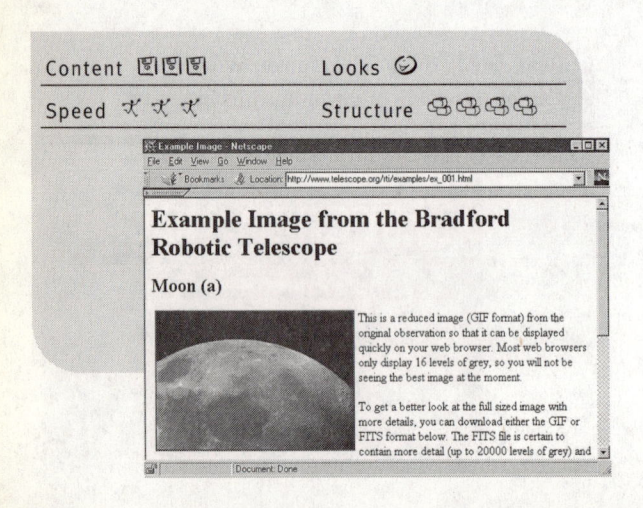

Content 🖼🖼🖼	Looks ☺
Speed ✗ ✗ ✗	Structure 🌀🌀🌀🌀

Example Image from the Bradford Robotic Telescope

Moon (a)

This is a reduced image (GIF format) from the original observation so that it can be displayed quickly on your web browser. Most web browsers only display 16 levels of grey, so you will not be seeing the best image at the moment.

To get a better look at the full sized image with more details, you can download either the GIF or FITS format below. The FITS file is certain to contain more detail (up to 20000 levels of grey) and

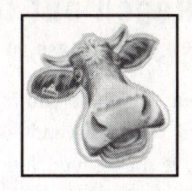

nine

Good Causes

The Web allows small organisations to be just as loud as multinational corporations so that charities and political groups can make their voices heard. The interactive nature of the Internet is also ideal for encouraging participation.

Reach out to youth

http://www.reachout.asn.au

Reach Out, an online youth-suicide prevention service, is one of the first Web-only charities in this country. It's a web site that 'listens'. It makes you feel important from the minute you arrive, allows you to personalise the look and feel of the site for your visit, and register it for next time. The graphics are gorgeous, the profiles inspirational, and the list of issues comprehensive. As well as the Chill Out section for youth, there are sections for family and friends who are concerned about the wellbeing of someone they know and for professionals looking for online resources.

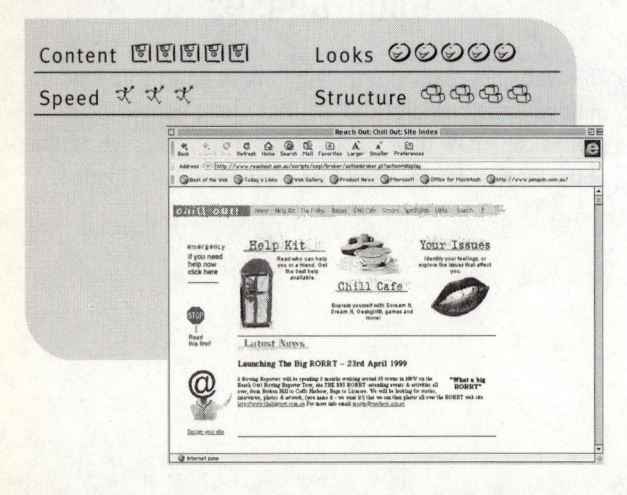

Content	📖📖📖📖📖	Looks	😊😊😊😊😊
Speed	✈✈✈	Structure	🐢🐢🐢🐢

A dog's life
http://www.guidedogs.com.au

Why do some blind people like dogs while others prefer a cane? The answer is at the Guide Dog Association site. Everything you ever wanted to know about vision impairment and dogs is here, complete with interviews (of people, not dogs) and a service directory. Find out if you have what it takes to be a puppywalker, try a crossword or order a guide dog beach towel.

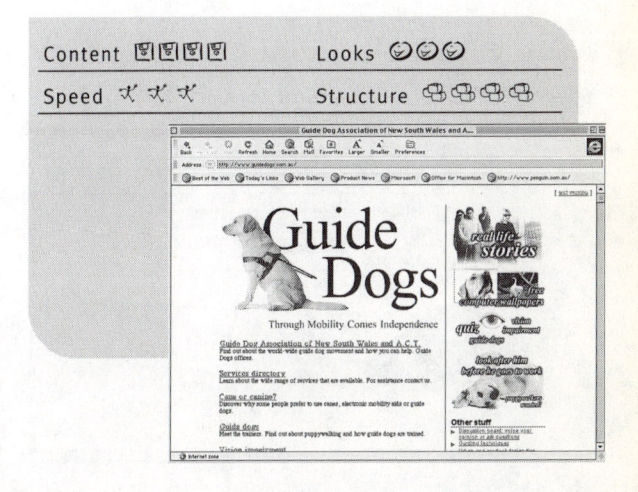

Content	🐕🐕🐕🐕	Looks	☺☺☺
Speed	🦴🦴🦴	Structure	🐾🐾🐾🐾

Conservation campaigns
http://www.acfonline.org.au

A national non-government environmental organisation, the Australian Conservation Foundation is currently campaigning against uranium mining and greenhouse gas emissions and for the protection of special natural places. You can order ACF calendars by printing out an online order form and faxing or posting it. Read their recent press releases; find out about membership, policies and other publications; or just flick through some of the beautiful images of Australian landscape and creatures dotted through the site.

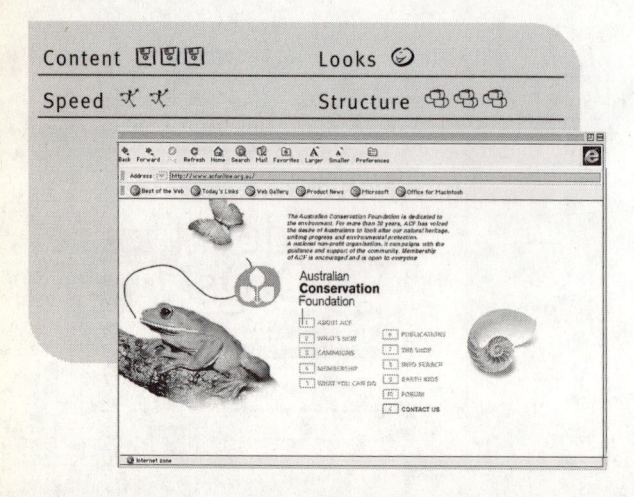

Content 📘📘📘	Looks 😊
Speed ✈✈	Structure 🌀🌀🌀

All creatures great and small
http://www.rspca.org.au

RSPCA Australia represents eight separate state and territory branches, most of which have their own sites. Find out where your nearest animal shelter is, get in touch with your local inspector if you have a problem, or contact and join a nearby branch. The very-slow-to-download British cousin, **www.rspca.org.uk**, lets you adopt a virtual pet. 'Play with it, feed it and watch it grow. If you treat it well, it will grow up to be strong, healthy and happy, but if you don't look after your Cyberpet, the RSPCA will come and take it away from you!' If only all pets were so lucky.

Content 🖫🖫🖫	Looks ☺
Speed ✄ ✄ ✄	Structure ꗃꗃꗃꗃ

Help communities abroad
http://www.caa.org.au

Community Aid Abroad aims to 'promote social justice and the alleviation of poverty through the funding of development projects both overseas and in Aboriginal Australia, and through our campaigning, education and advocacy work'. Besides the usual information on current campaigns and how to make a donation, the CAA site features a selection of delicious-sounding vegetarian recipes from around the world and an online version of its catalogue so you can order jewellery, clothes, books, calendars, furniture, baskets and more in the name of a good cause.

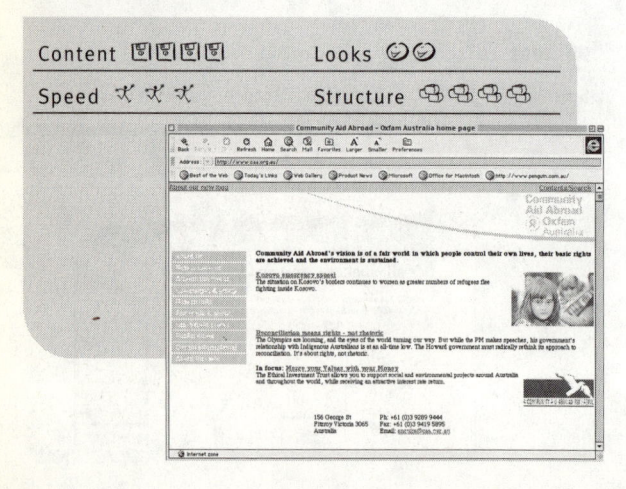

Content 🖻🖻🖻🖻	Looks ☺☺
Speed ✈ ✈ ✈	Structure ♘♘♘♘

The Salvos
http://www.salvos.org.au

It's not easy walking past one of those smiling grandfatherly Salvation Army types without giving him your loose change to help the Salvos continue their work in the community. The music isn't too bad either. The official web site is a useful starting point for people who are interested in the Salvos' work, or just want to find out when they can catch the next concert, fete or other event. Like the Salvation Army International Millennial Congress, to be held in Atlanta in 2000. Imagine all those uniforms and tambourines in one place!

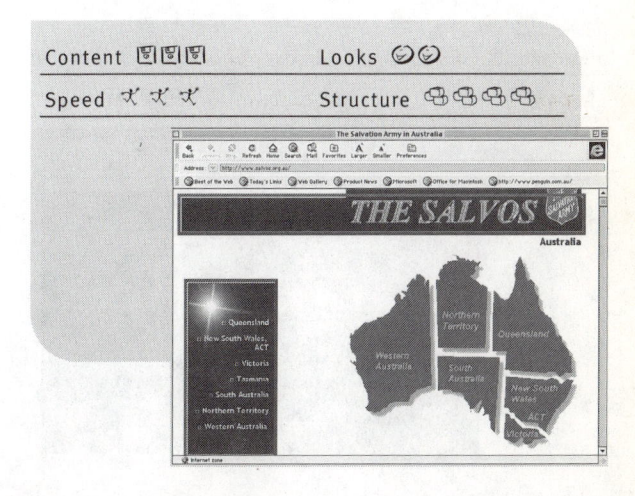

Content 🖻🖻🖻	Looks ☺☺
Speed ✶✶✶	Structure ♧♧♧♧

Human rights
http://www.amnesty.org.au

On Human Rights Day 1998, the 50th anniversary of the Universal Declaration of Human Rights, Amnesty Australia's web site had collected around 335 000 pledges of support for human rights (including those submitted following an email appeal). They were added to ten million pledges collected by Amnesty International, and presented to the United Nations in Paris on the big day. The sophisticated web site provides information on joining, the latest campaigns and more.

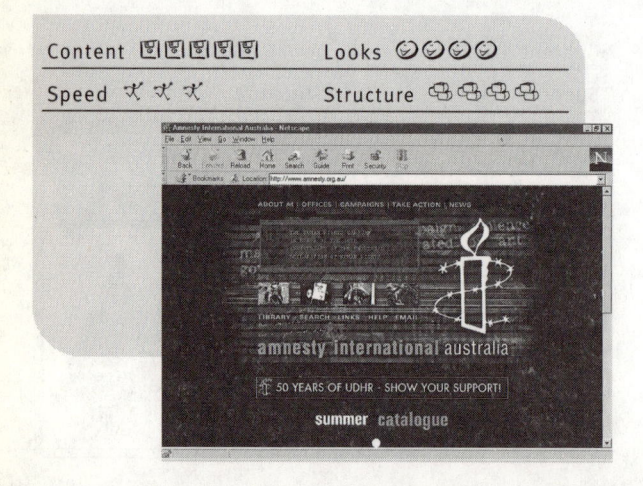

Content 🖼🖼🖼🖼🖼	Looks ☺☺☺☺
Speed ✈✈✈	Structure 🕸🕸🕸🕸

Apologise to the stolen generations

http://apology.west.net.au

Another good cause that has made excellent use of the interactive nature of the Web to promote itself is that of Aboriginal reconciliation. Visitors to the Stolen Generations site enter their details electronically to 'sign' a petition: 'We, the undersigned people of Australia, believe an apology is owed to those of our fellow citizens who were separated from their families as a direct result of government policy. We offer that apology.' The site also provides links to dozens of other online publications relating to Aboriginal reconciliation and native title.

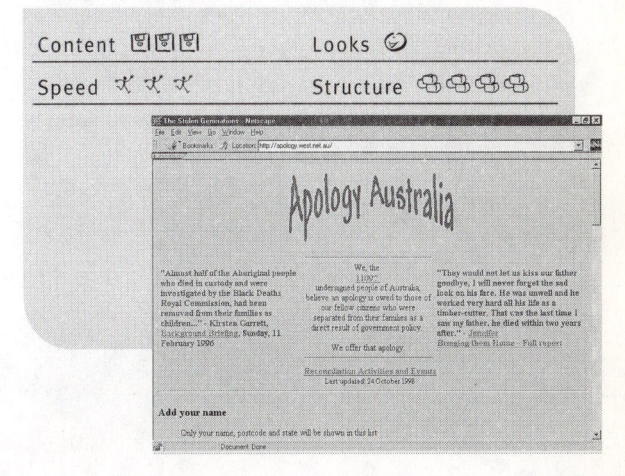

Content 📖📖📖	Looks 😊
Speed ✈✈✈	Structure 🔗🔗🔗🔗

Here comes the Republic

http://www.republic.org.au

My loyalty to the so-called mother country goes as far as preferring *Yes Minister* and *This Life* to *Spin City* and *Friends*. Beyond that, I'd have to say that despite my Anglo-Celtic origins I am an Australian, and I'd like to have a head of state who feels the same way. It's only fair that I point you to the Australians for Constitutional Monarchy site too: **www.norepublic.com.au**.

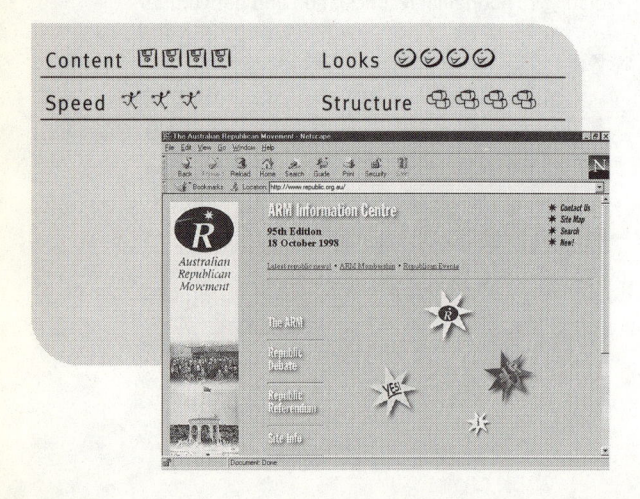

Content	Looks
Speed	Structure

A new flag

http://www.ausflag.com.au

Ausflag is an 'apolitical, non-profit organisation seeking to secure the popular support of the Australian people for the adoption of a truly Australian flag'. They haven't had much luck so far, partly because of the strong historical ties many Australians feel to the existing flag. I suspect it's only a matter of time, though, before the Union Jack disappears from one of our most important national symbols. Have a look at the 100 finalists in a professional design competition held in 1998. They were all posted on the Ausflag site, where visitors were able to vote for their favourite design online.

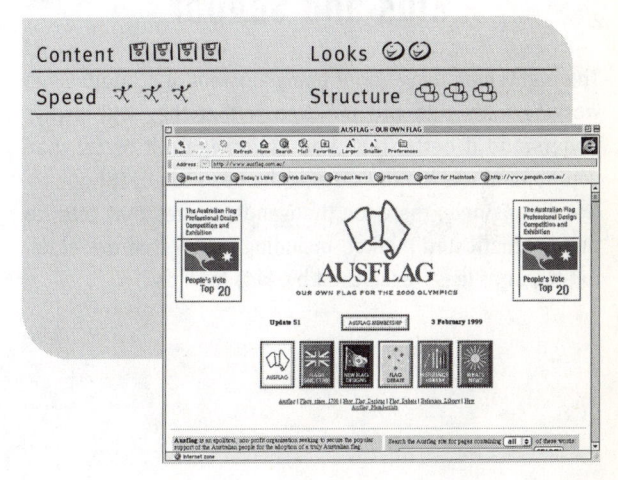

Content 🖾🖾🖾🖾	Looks 😊😊
Speed ✈✈✈	Structure ♣♣♣

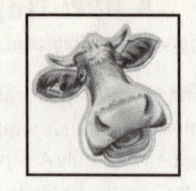

ten

Kids and School

The frightening thing about being a parent or schoolteacher working with kids and the Web is that they will always understand it better than you do, navigate it better than you do, and use it more cleverly than you can ever hope to. Not surprisingly, there are thousands of sites that cater to this sophisticated market, including plenty that are either run by, or at least researched by, kids for kids.

Cultural exchange
http://www.iefaust.org.au

The International Education Forum organises secondary student exchanges, guaranteeing visits to participants' country of choice. Their mission? To encourage improved foreign language skills, knowledge of the host country, tolerance and understanding. 'Students can study overseas for a short term, a semester or the whole school year and overseas students spend five or eleven months living with Australian families.' The site features multilingual guides, student stories and a parents' page.

Content	📖📖📖📖	Looks	☺☺☺☺
Speed	✈✈✈✈	Structure	✢✢✢

Email penpals
http://topnet.com.au/epals.html

Topnet's kids' site provides a list of potential penpals, divided by age from 5 to 19, from all around the world. And for parents worried about where this could lead, don't be. The site is littered with sensible advice such as this: 'It is very important that you understand what NOT to put on message boards like this. Sadly, some people might want to use this information for their own good and not care whether it annoys or hurts anyone else. So please, be careful. NEVER GIVE: Your last name, your street, any phone number, school or parents' work.'

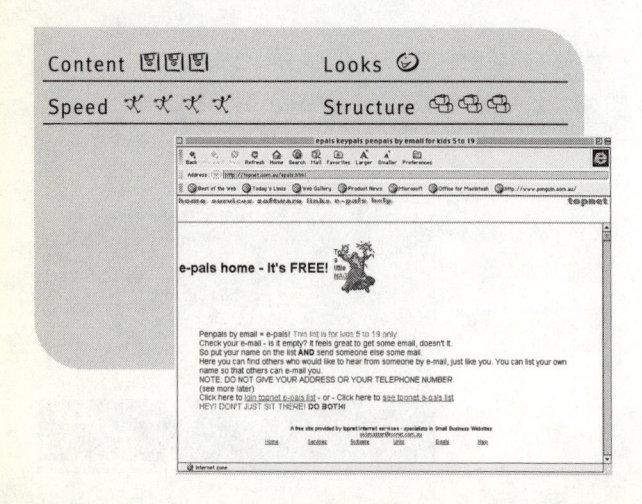

Content 🖳🖳🖳	Looks ☺
Speed ✗ ✗ ✗ ✗	Structure ✿✿✿

Online gardening
http://www.nickoz.com

Online Treehouse, the Australian web site of kids' pay-TV channel Nickelodeon, has become a regular haunt for more than 5000 registered online gardeners. They're virtual gardeners, working with virtual spades, fountains, gnomes, birdhouses, ponds, trees, plants and changing weather to create their own individual piece of cyberhorticulture. It's like a tamagotchi, but less predictable. When you get to the site, click on the Treehouse and on to the Online Garden. Enter your details to collect a password, then wait a couple of minutes for the Shockwave garden to appear. Happy digging.

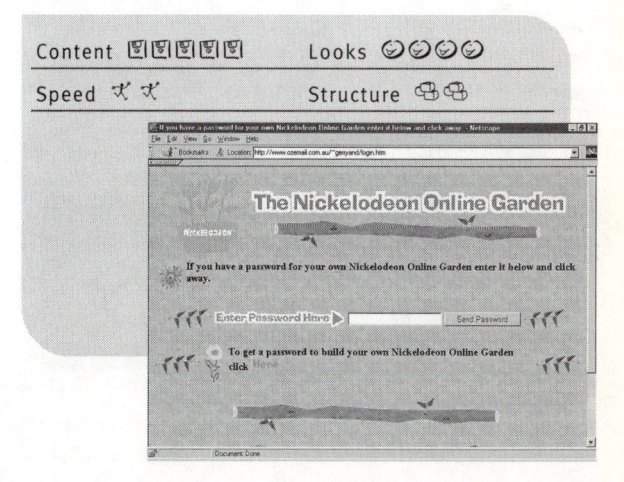

Content	🖼🖼🖼🖼	Looks	😊😊😊😊
Speed	✈ ✈	Structure	❀❀

Proof it
http://www.correctme.com

If you're an HSC student needing help with essay proofreading or a uni student from a non-English-speaking background, or you just want someone to cast an experienced eye over your Microsoft Word documents before you print them, Correct Me may be for you. It's a service run by professional linguists and experienced English-language teachers. The team at Correct Me will proofread, edit and correct essays and letters using 100 or so hyperlinks explaining grammatical errors. These are embedded into submitted works and paid for by secure credit-card transactions.

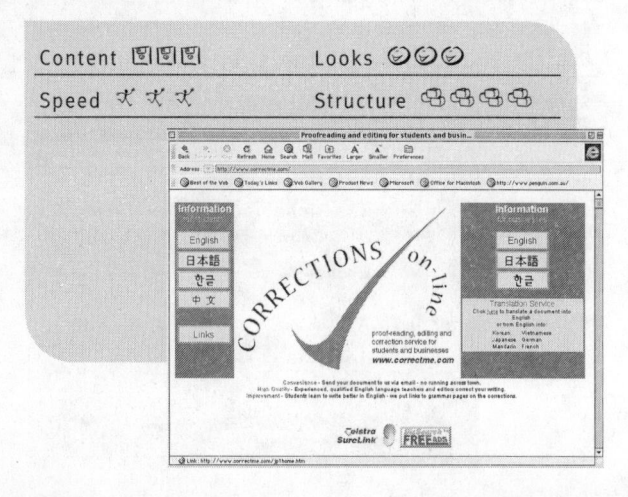

Stuff from the kitchen
http://freeweb.pdq.net/headstrong/

A perfect site for science teachers desperately seeking groovy ways to keep students awake. It calls itself 'an ever-growing warehouse of the kinds of projects some of the more demented of us tried as young people'. It's a sort of warped, semi-scientific cookbook of tricks, gimmicks and pointless experimentation, concoctions and devices using, for the most part, things found around the house. Strange goo, radios made from rusty razor blades, crystal gardens – amateur mad-scientist stuff. Try the pinhole camera, electric magnets or non-dairy creamer ballistics.

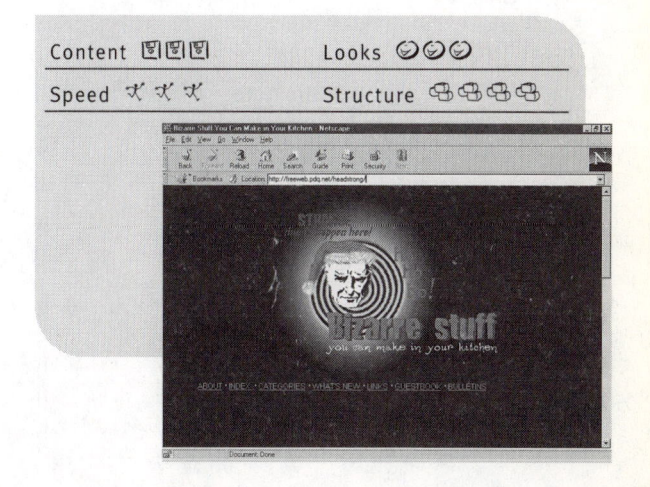

Content	📖📖📖	Looks	☺☺☺
Speed	✈✈✈	Structure	🏛🏛🏛🏛

Race across time

http://www.phm.gov.au/rat/

The Powerhouse Museum has joined forces with AT&T to create an interactive online game designed to help 8 to 14-year-olds learn about technology, geography and history. Kids hop in the driving seat of a time-cruiser and go looking for clues. Explore the Powerhouse's site while you're there. It might inspire a real school-holiday visit.

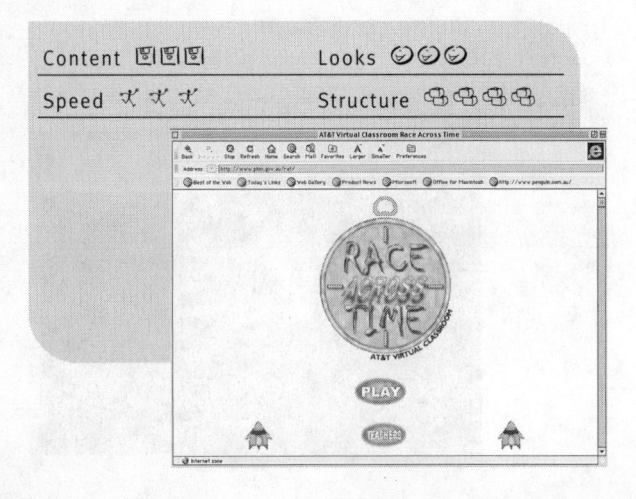

Content 🖻🖻🖻	Looks 😊😊😊
Speed ✰✰✰	Structure 🐌🐌🐌🐌

Community of kids
http://www.kahootz.com.au

Kahootz is a kids-only online community administered by Telstra, Hewlett-Packard and the Australian Children's Television Foundation. It's not possible to join by visiting the web site: you also need a copy of the CD-ROM (details are on site) and a password. Once ready to join, you create your own icon, which is how others will see you in the Kahootz environment. Parents will like Kahootz because it will entertain the kids for hours on a regular basis, and because it's not connected to the rest of the Web. That means kids can't access public sites from Kahootz, and can only email other Kahootz members.

Content 🖳🖳🖳🖳	Looks 😊😊😊😊
Speed ✈ ✈ ✈	Structure 🏶🏶🏶🏶

Tubbythumping

http://www.bbc.co.uk/education/teletubbies/

At the BBC *Teletubbies* site fans can play Shockwave games such as Time for Tubby Bye Bye and Noo-Noo Tidies Up, colour them in using a virtual paintbrush, or read the section of tips for parents and carers. (By the way, I disagree with their advice to never leave your child on the Net unsupervised; if you set up their bookmarks carefully, they're safer there than in front of a television set.) For Tubby-cynicism, visit the Official Teletubbies Conspiracy Site at **www.mtattersall.demon.co.uk/tubbies/home.html**.

Content 🖳🖳🖳🖳	Looks 😊😊😊😊
Speed ✈✈	Structure 🌐🌐

Ultimate Disney fun

http://www.disney.com

Disney's site is so loaded with entertainment, information, multimedia and interactivity, you won't know where to start. Unfortunately some of the best kids' stuff requires registering and paying by credit card, but not all of it does. Watch video bloopers from the latest Disney film, hear Radio Disney, catch live events or explore the rest of the Web using Disney's family Internet guide.

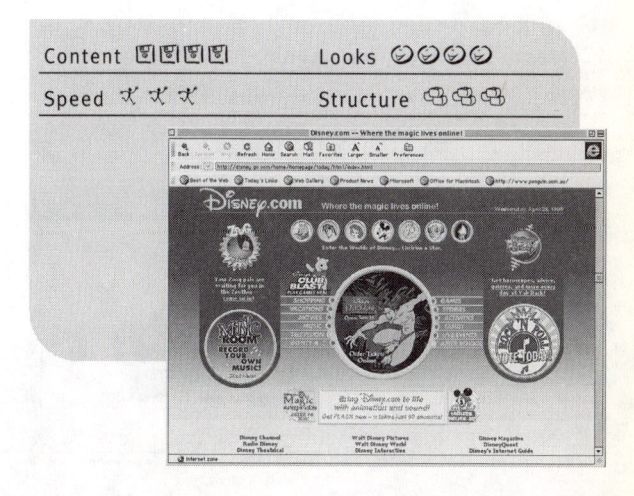

Content
Looks
Speed
Structure

Morphs and bumps
http://www.scholastic.com.au/kidszone/

Into Goosebumps at all? Or Animorphs? The slow and noisy Animorphs site at Scholastic means business. No little Shockwave games here. Instead, download a full interactive game and instructions, full-screen pictures, morphing screensavers or desktop patterns and video clips. Both the Animorphs and Goosebumps sites offer a choice between high and low bandwidth versions.

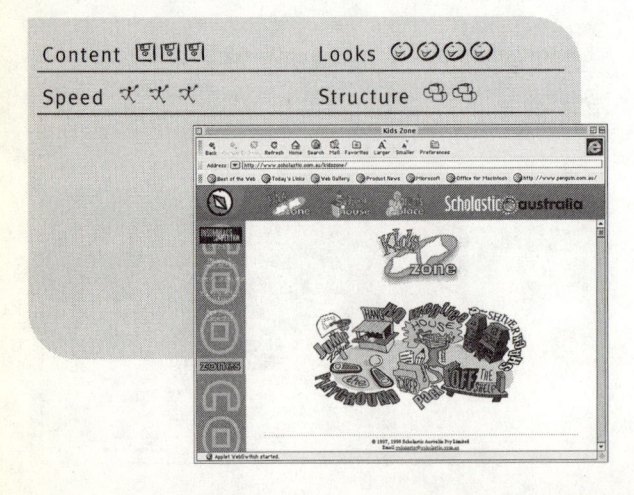

Content 📖📖📖	Looks 😊😊😊😊
Speed ✈✈✈	Structure 🧩🧩

Dinosaur info
http://headlines.yahoo.com/Full_Coverage/Yahooligans/dinosaurs

Yahooligans' dinosaur page is better than any old dinosaur site because it points you to the best information and multimedia related to dinosaurs wherever it is on the Web. Read about dinosaur egg hatching, a fossil that links dinosaurs and birds, and the meteor that may have killed off the giant creatures.

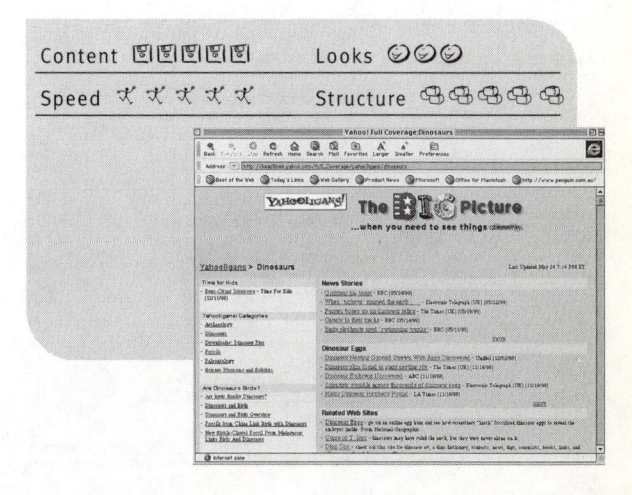

Content 📖📖📖📖📖 Looks 😊😊😊

Speed ✈✈✈✈✈ Structure 🌐🌐🌐🌐🌐

The FBI's X-files
http://www.fbi.gov/foipa/main.htm

The FBI Freedom of Information Act Home Page includes an electronic reading room of old case files. In the Famous Persons section you'll find accounts of Marilyn Monroe's alleged affairs and speculation about the circumstances surrounding her death alongside files on John Lennon and John Wayne. You'll need to download the Acrobat Reader (the site provides a link) and be patient (the FBI denies it has purposely made the documents slow to access). Files relating to UFO cases are in the Unusual Phenomena section, or try Espionage, Violent Crime, the Gangster Era or Historical Interest.

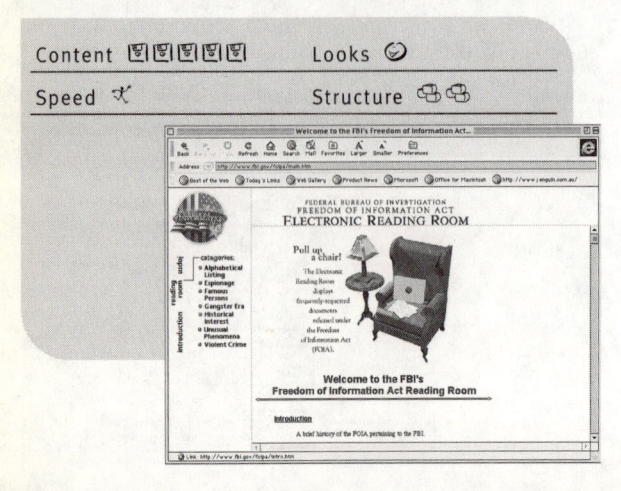

Content 🖳🖳🖳🖳🖳	Looks ☺
Speed ✈	Structure 🕸🕸

Fressshhhhh fruit

http://www.fandvforme.com.au

The graphics at this site are as good as any you'll find. The Sydney Markets and NSW Fresh Fruit and Vegetable Industry people behind it consulted kids when creating it, and the information (which covers recipes, the history, growing areas, nutritional value and varieties of more than 60 different fruits or vegetables) is the kind we would have paid good pocket money for when we had school projects to do.

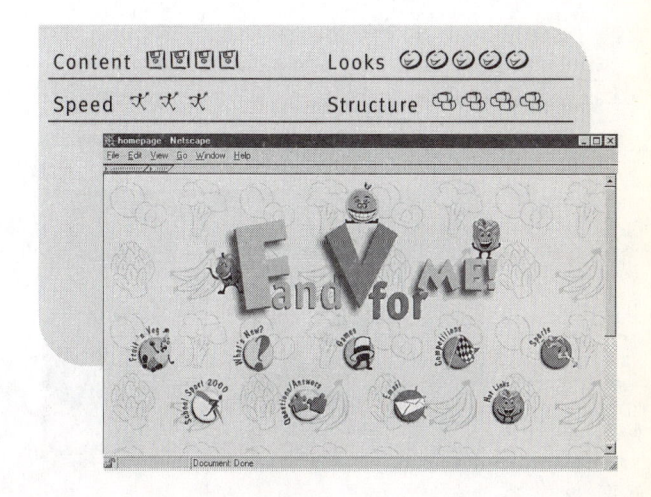

Content 🖳🖳🖳🖳	Looks 😊😊😊😊😊
Speed ✈ ✈ ✈	Structure 🜲🜲🜲🜲

A rose in every cheek

http://www.vegemite.com.au

Did you know Vegemite was invented in 1922 by a young chemist named Dr Cyril P. Callister, at the Fred Walker Cheese Company? The Vege-site's Time Machine takes you back through the decades of Vegemite history. Kids can also keep track of their growth by recording their height each time they visit, learn about nutrition, sing along to the 'Happy Little Vegemites' tune and try recipes featuring Australia's favourite spread.

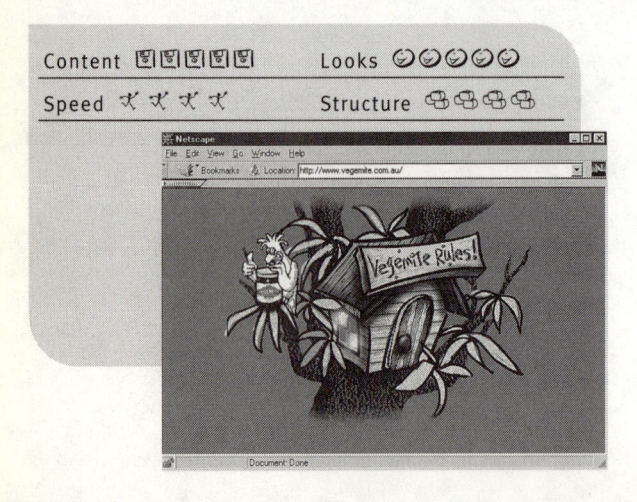

Content 📖📖📖📖📖 Looks 😊😊😊😊😊
Speed ✈✈✈✈ Structure 🐢🐢🐢🐢

Didge you know?
Aboriginal facts

http://www.aboriginalaustralia.com.au

This site is described by its backers as 'an ethical business venture underpinned by culturally approval protocols [and] respect for Aboriginal intellectual property rights'. It's 50 per cent owned by Aborigines, and features a bookstore with 400 titles relating to Aboriginality. Many of these can be ordered through **amazon.com**. There are also sections on art, eco-travel and spirituality, all complemented by beautiful photography and Aboriginal designs.

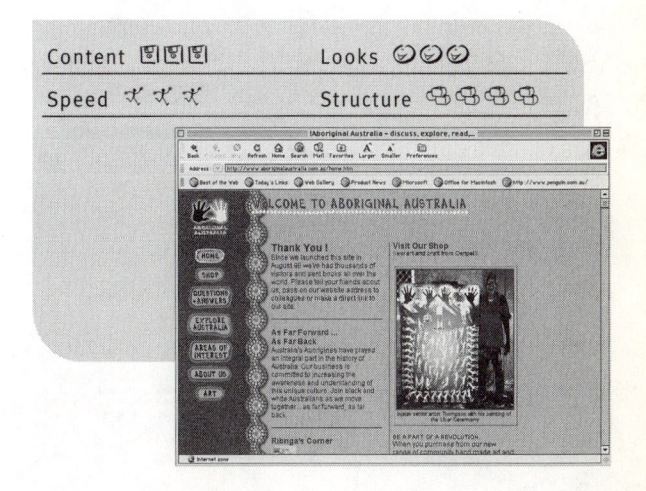

Content 圖圖圖	Looks ☺☺☺
Speed ✈✈✈	Structure ♘♘♘♘

Languages of the world
http://gamma.sil.org/ethnologue/

The Ethnologue (maintained by the Summer Institute of Linguistics) catalogues more than 6700 languages spoken in 228 countries. Search through the index according to language family, geographical area or language name. English slots into the Indo-European category, in the Germanic branch. Its closest relative is a language called Frisian, spoken in parts of Germany and the Netherlands.

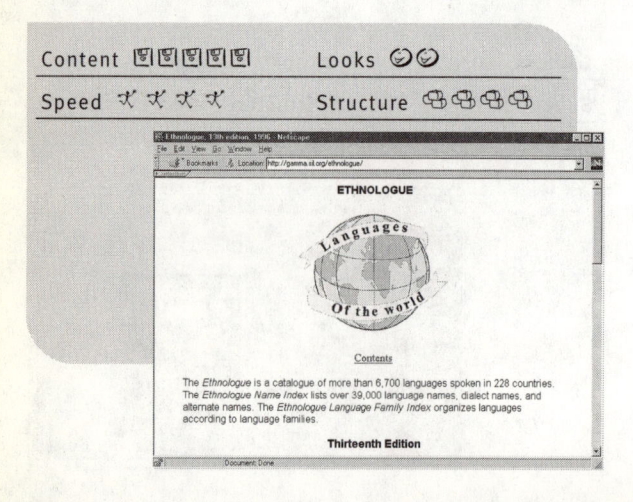

Content	🗒🗒🗒🗒🗒	Looks	😊😊
Speed	✗ ✗ ✗ ✗	Structure	🧩🧩🧩🧩

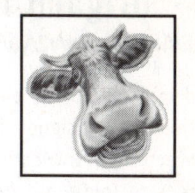

eleven

DIY

The multimedia capabilities of web sites make them far superior to do-it-yourself books, while the text-based elements make them superior to DIY TV. You can learn music theory or ballroom dancing, brush up on your Latin, or pursue a new hobby, all online.

Origami fanciers
http://io360.com/v2/yo/iogami/

Find yourself a pretty piece of paper and sit down for a session at this site, designed by a New York-based studio. Choose between four intricately constructed birds, each requiring dozens of folds, but demonstrated clearly using Shockwave Flash technology.

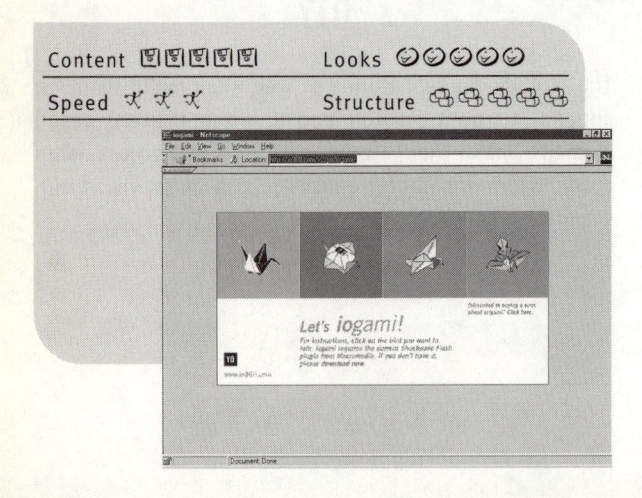

Dance hall dazzlers
http://www.ballroomdancers.com

Take a step-by-step course in the waltz, tango, foxtrot or salsa. This web site demonstrates basic steps using charts, video clips and photos. Try the variation of the month or join a discussion on dance. There are technical tips and a glossary of terms, too.

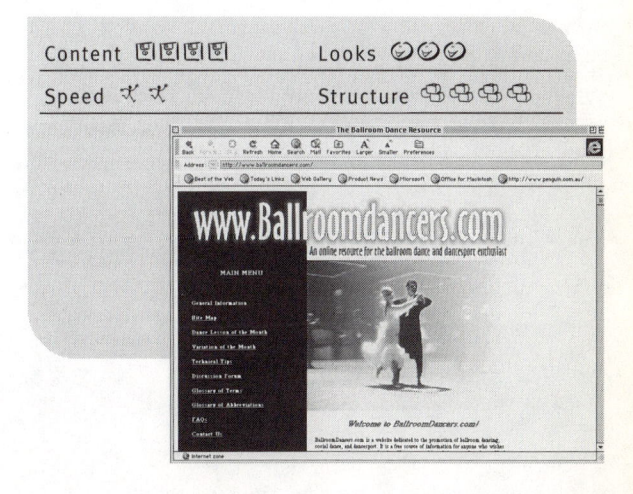

Content	🖼🖼🖼🖼	Looks	☺☺☺
Speed	✧ ✧	Structure	♧♧♧♧

Green thumbs

http://www.global-garden.com.au

Global Garden is a free online magazine for Australians and people gardening in similar climates, like California. Check out the planters' guide, landscaping tips, book reviews and list of links (including the Gardening Launch Pad, which points you to more than 2000 gardening sites, and the Society for Growing Australian Plants). Email your less-than-green-thumb queries to the editor, and subscribe to be notified of site updates.

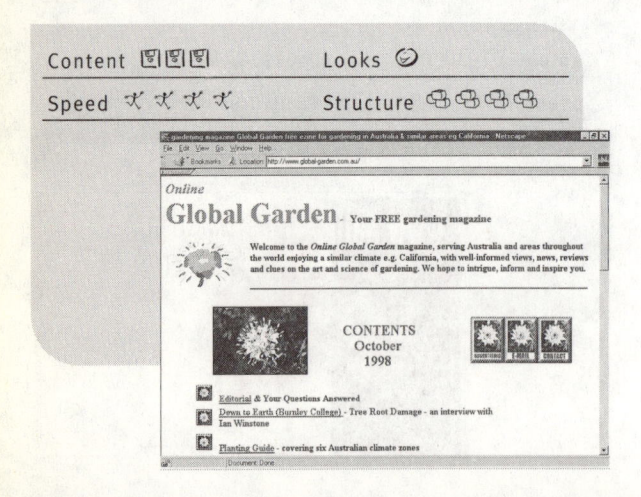

Content 📖📖📖	Looks ☺
Speed ✗✗✗✗	Structure ☁☁☁☁

Personal trainer
http://www.bfit.net

If you're spending a lot of time online, you probably need to walk away from the PC and do some exercise, so why not find the inspiration on the Web? The message of the week when we visited BFIT was 'Add life to your years, not years to your life – be fit'. This is the site that tells you how to plan your fitness program. Read up on workout routines, health and exercise issues, sports injury, travel fitness tips, nutrition and diet, and the personal trainer's perspective. The only downside to BFIT (apart from the dinky graphics) is that it costs to subscribe – but the fee is nowhere near as much as your local gym or golf club.

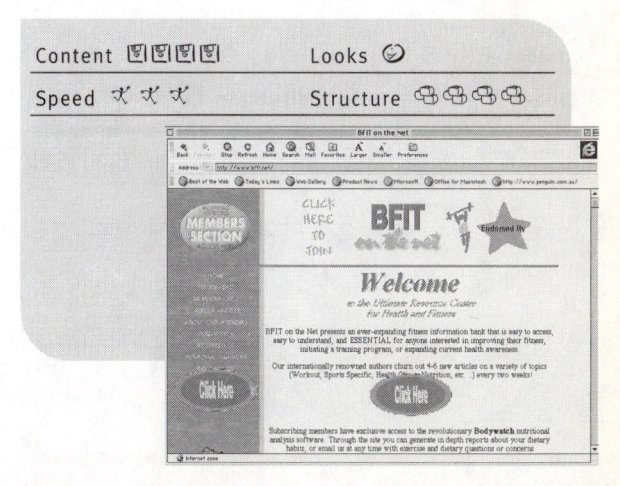

Content	📖📖📖📖	Looks	☺
Speed	✈ ✈ ✈	Structure	🏛🏛🏛🏛

Musical notes

http://www.nor.com.au/community/musicmagic/

Australian site Music Magic could slot into the music section of this book, but its DIY music theory and guitar lessons make it a perfect fit for this collection of sites. Learn about Every Good Boy Deserves Fruit, the treble clef, the guitar fret board and the world of MIDI (Musical Instrument Digital Interface).

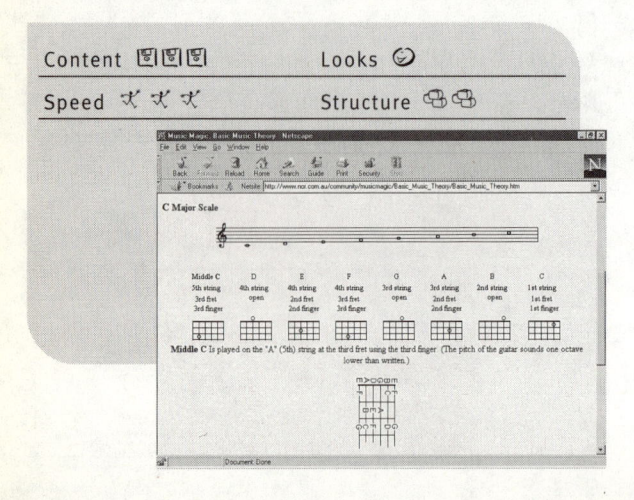

Content 📖📖📖	Looks 😊
Speed ✈ ✈ ✈	Structure 🔗🔗

Quit smoking
http://www.smokenders.com

There are few better feelings than the sense of empowerment gained by quitting smoking. Smokenders did it for me. They make sure you stop by charging you a one-off fortune to sit around in an unventilated room with heavy-smoking, half-dead, long-term smokers ashing in overflowing ashtrays once a week until you stop. Oh, but that's not all. They also make you keep all your butts in a jar to give you an idea of how much nicotine you're pumping into your system. The organisation's flashy web site contains lots of information on the perils of smoking and how you can stop.

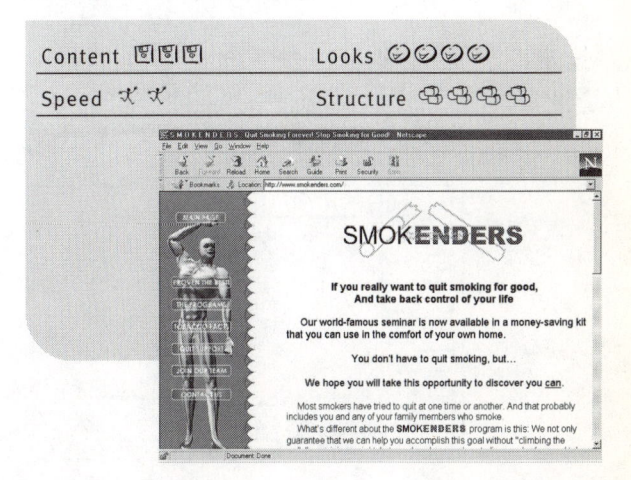

Content 📖📖📖	Looks ☺☺☺☺
Speed �✶	Structure ♧♧♧♧

Gnocchi with four cheeses
http://www.tamaraskitchen.com.au

Tamara's Kitchen is an Australian site for food lovers, which is great because it uses Aussie terminology, ingredients and measurements (and features a conversion table and glossary of terms). Send Tamara Milstein your cooking questions, find out when she's teaching in your area, order utensils and gourmet foods, or just choose a recipe to print out – how about herbed pumpkin gnocchi with a four-cheese sauce tonight?

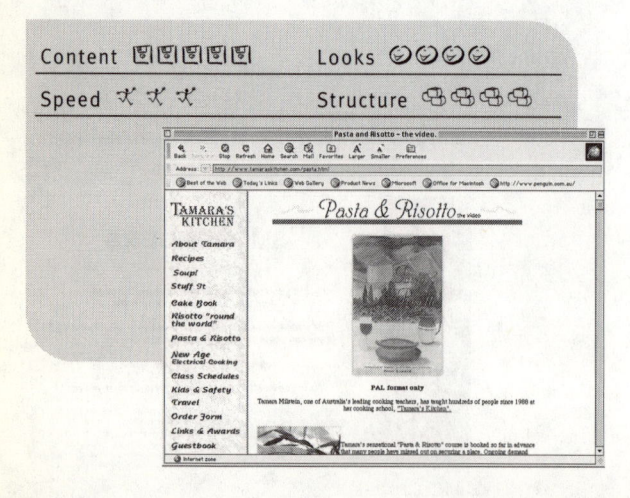

Content	Looks
Speed	Structure

Home handyperson

http://www.naturalhandyman.com/iip/iip.htm

Whether you need help repairing a clothes dryer or squeaky door, dealing with rats, painting walls, or fixing or improving just about anything you can think of around the house, Natural Handyman's Home Repair Index is the place to visit for information. If you're really into home improvement, sign up to receive the site's regular newsletter. If you're hopeless around the house and need help with a particular issue the site doesn't cover, email your query to the Natural.

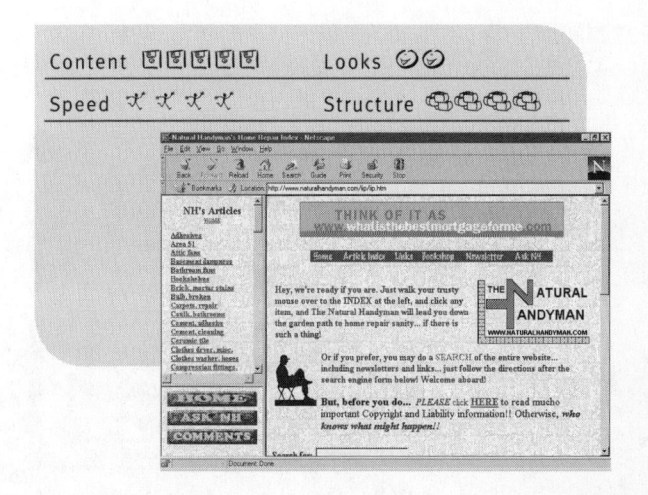

Content ▨▨▨▨▨   Looks ☺☺
Speed ✄✄✄✄   Structure ✇✇✇✇✇

You want to learn? This is the place

http://www.learn2.com

This site can teach you just about anything you want to know, from taking a free throw in basketball to taking a pulse. There are thousands of '2torials' which explain, in detail, what to do and how to do it. One for the bookmarks.

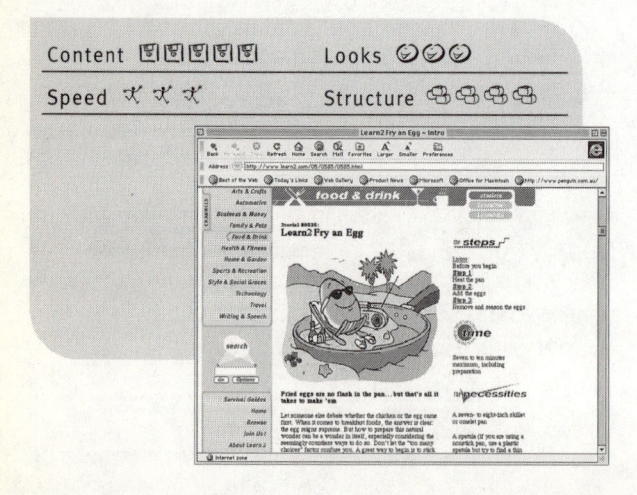

Content 📖📖📖📖	Looks 😊😊😊
Speed ✈✈✈	Structure 🖱🖱🖱🖱

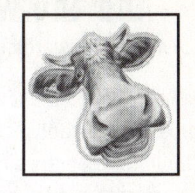

twelve

Awards

The Web industry is just as keen to congratulate itself as the people who make movies, so you'll find plenty of award sites and competitions devoted to the online medium. The most fun awards are those that allow Web users to participate by voting and sending in their own nominations. For example, in 1998 Hank the angry, drunken dwarf managed to pip Leonardo DiCaprio at the post in *People* Online's most beautiful people poll (www.pathfinder.com/people/50most/1998/vote/latestresults.html).

And the winner is...
http://www.webawards.info.au

The *Australian Financial Review*/Telstra Australian Internet Awards have established themselves as the Web awards that matter in this country since they were first held in 1996. Anyone can nominate a site, but it must be Australian to qualify. In 1998, public voting for nominated sites closed in August, and the awards ceremony took place in November. The organisers are creating something of an annual snapshot of the best of the Web, compiling an archive of each year's best sites in their respective categories. It's a great place to visit to get a feel for what Aussie Web gurus (of all ages and budgets) are capable of.

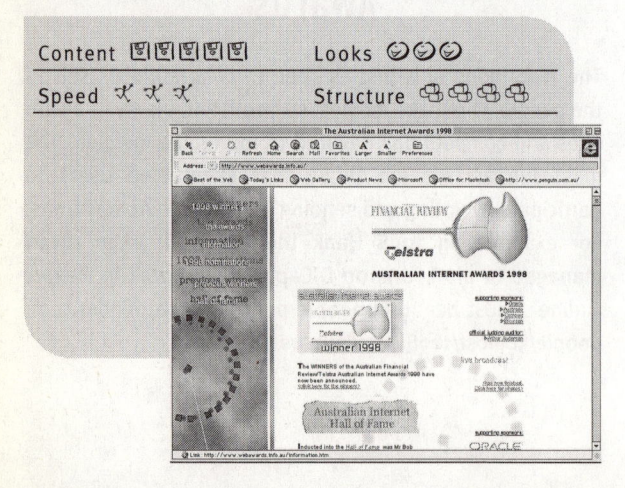

Content 🖹🖹🖹🖹🖹	Looks ☺☺☺
Speed ✈ ✈ ✈	Structure ♋♋♋♋

Schools Web competition
http://www.learning21.org

Each year Australian primary and secondary students have an opportunity to prove how much better they are at Web design than their parents, older siblings and professional counterparts, while giving their schools the chance to share in more than $50 000 in prizes. Their brief in 1998: to find a hot issue in their area that has been solved in a clever manner, use the Net to find out if another place in the world faces a similar problem, and create a site to explain the solution. Visit the competition site to check out recent winners – the site developers of the future.

Content 📖📖📖	Looks 😊😊
Speed ✈ ✈ ✈	Structure 🗂🗂

Razzies

http://www.razzies.com

The Golden Raspberry Award Foundation presents an entertaining antidote for those who've had Hollywood's Oscarfest up to here: 'While the "real Academy" wracks its brains trying to find even *five* good films that were made this year, why not take a look at the other 500 *bad* films of the year, and their award . . . the Razzie'. Join the crew of film professionals, journalists and movie fans who nominate and vote in the Razzies each year. By the way, they're announced the day before the Oscars, and the winners are encouraged to accept a gold-painted, golfball-sized plastic raspberry atop a super-eight film reel trophy.

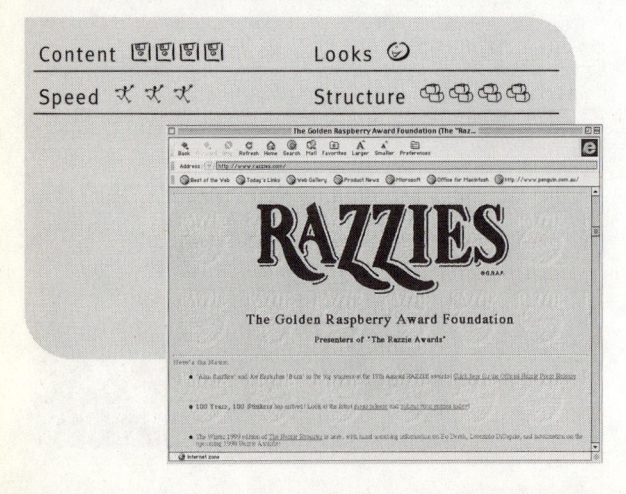

Content 📺📺📺📺	Looks ☺
Speed ✗✗✗	Structure 🌀🌀🌀🌀

Bobbies

http://www.go2net.com/internet/useless/useless/bobbies98.html

The Bobbie Awards are named after 'Microsoft Bob, a piece of software so useless even Microsoft's marketing folks couldn't sell it'. They celebrate all that is totally useless in cyberspace. Find out who holds the crown for Useless *Star Wars* Page (*Star Wars* Stick Figures at **www.infinityrealm.com/stick.html**) or overall Useless Site of the Year. Previous years' awards links are archived, but not surprisingly, many of the useless sites they refer to are long gone. *C'est la vie* in the online world.

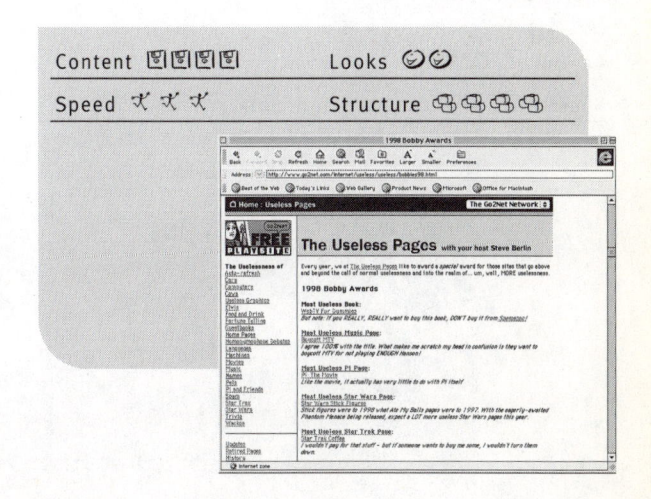

Content 🗒️🗒️🗒️🗒️ Looks 😊😊

Speed ✈️✈️✈️ Structure 🏛️🏛️🏛️🏛️

Webbies

http://www.webbies.com

The Webbies are the San Francisco multimedia set's answer to LA's Oscars. They're divided into two sections: those voted on by a group called the International Academy of Digital Arts and Sciences (the Webbies), and the People's Voice Awards. Both are awarded in 24 categories, including arts, commerce, fashion, film, games, health, humour, music, news, politics and law, print and zines, radio, science, search engines and portals, sports, TV, travel and weird. Scanning through 1998's winners will lead to hours of happy Web surfing – there are some fantastic sites listed.

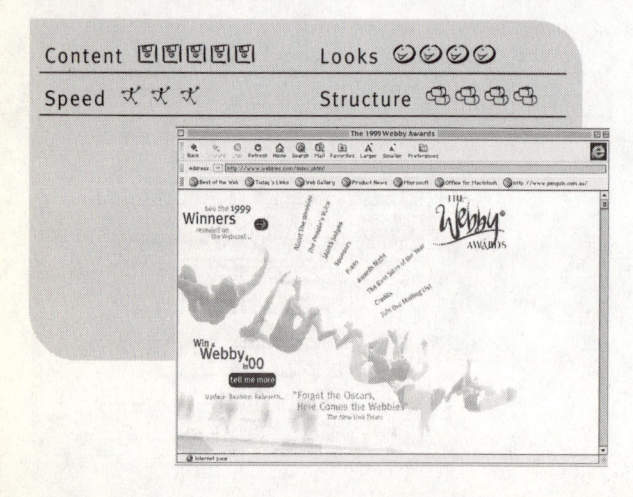

Content	📖📖📖📖📖	Looks	😊😊😊😊
Speed	✈✈✈	Structure	⌘⌘⌘⌘

Time 100 poll
http://cgi.pathfinder.com/time/time100/poc/century.html

When we visited, Jesus Christ was sitting in first place. Adolf Hitler was second. Where? *Time* magazine's Person of the Century online poll, which includes discussion, a quiz, bulletin boards and lots of historical information. Anyone can vote, as evidenced by the number five ranking: Mustafa Kemal Ataturk. Turkey's Net population was reportedly encouraged by the Turkish government to visit the site and put in a vote for Ataturk. Oh, and *South Park*'s Eric Cartman was sitting in third place. No lie.

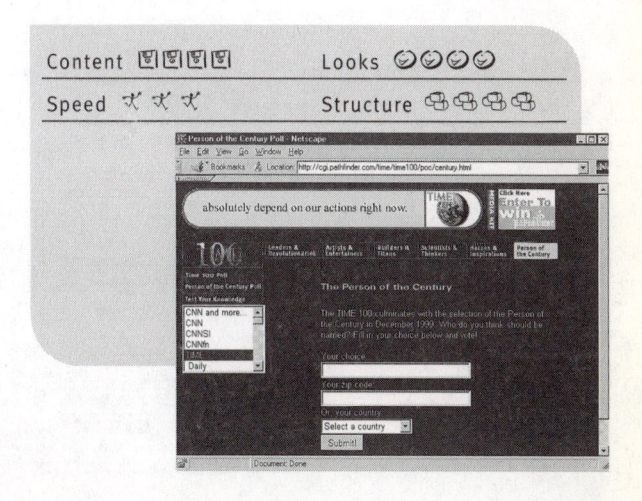

Content 😐😐😐😐 Looks 😊😊😊😊
Speed ✈ ✈ ✈ Structure 🕸🕸🕸🕸

Darwin Awards
http://www.darwinawards.com

Since 1992, the Darwin Awards have commemorated those who made the ultimate sacrifice by eliminating themselves from the species in an extraordinarily novel fashion, thereby improving our genetic pool. The Kansas woman who allowed her ten-year-old son to back the family car down the drive and was run down and killed when he stepped on the accelerator instead of the brakes is just one example. You won't know whether to laugh or cry.

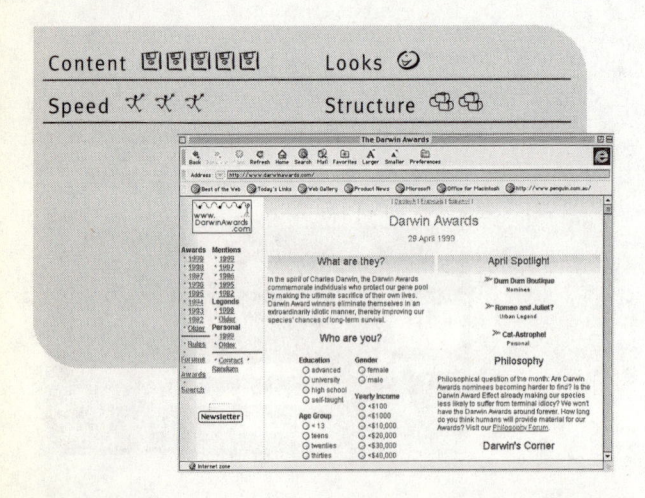

Content	🎖🎖🎖🎖🎖	Looks	☺
Speed	✗ ✗ ✗	Structure	🐛🐛

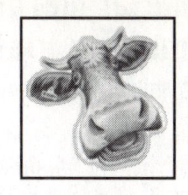

thirteen

Truly Weird

Sometimes it may not be a good thing that the Web allows anyone with a hare-brained scheme to promote themselves globally. We could do without scary neo-Nazis, for starters. But for the most part the bizarre and peculiar stuff you find online is harmless. Dead people's memoirs, religious fanatics' ravings, trivia and memorabilia sites – they're all here. Go to a search engine and type in just about any zany idea you can think of, and there'll be a site for it. Let's try 'beachcombing' at Yahoo. Bingo! Up pops 'Steven Miller's Beachcombing Page – tips for beachcombers, with a focus on Japanese glass floats'. What's a Japanese glass float anyway?

Metal merchants: number plates of the world

http://danshiki.oit.gatech.edu/~iadt3mk/

Believe it. This site is devoted to number plates from around the world. Use the world map to find the plates you're most interested in. If the world is strange enough to use sheets of metal to distinguish cars and drivers, why not set up a site to compare them?

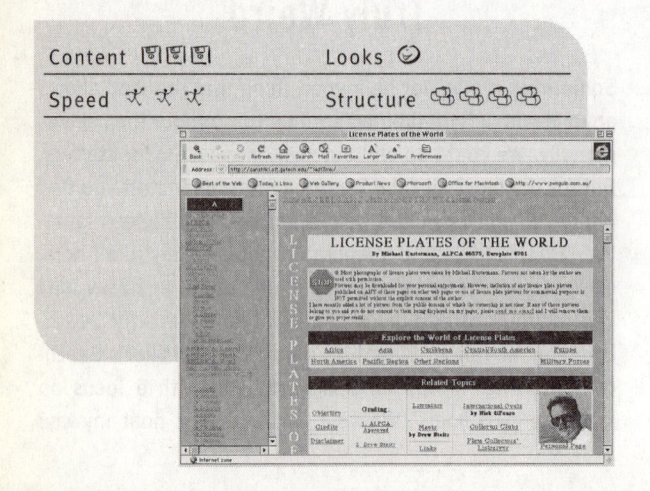

Content 📖📖📖	Looks 😊
Speed 🏃 🏃 🏃	Structure 🌀🌀🌀🌀

Name-calling
http://www.kabalarians.com/gkh/your.htm

'Although your name of Charlotte has created an expressive, fun-loving nature, it has not produced the qualities necessary for a full and complete life.' Well, that's it, then. Might as well throw in the towel here and now. No – incomplete as it may be, it's all worth it when we find entertaining and entirely useless sites such as this, which claims that 'The more insight you have into the powerful influence of your name, the greater opportunity to enjoy the success you are capable of achieving'. It analyses hundreds of names, suggesting health problem areas, personality traits and romantic possibilities for each.

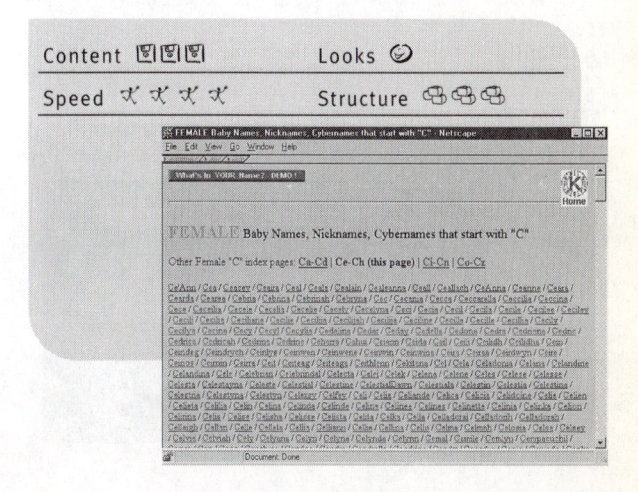

Content 📖📖📖 Looks 😊

Speed ✈✈✈✈ Structure ⚙⚙⚙

Christians for cloning Jesus
http://www.geocities.com/Athens/Acropolis/8611/page2.htm

This crowd has set up a page to proclaim the fact that the end of the world is nigh and it's just way too late to sit and wait for the second coming. We should take action now and use samples from the Shroud of Turin to clone Jesus. Hell, this lot goes so far as to suggest that every home should have its own personal Jesus. Click on the lamb link while you're there to get a feel for what these people really think.

Content 📖📖	Looks 😊😊
Speed 🏃🏃🏃🏃	Structure 🐑🐑

Subtitles and Japanese snacks

http://www.rotodesign.com/subtitles/subtitles.html
http://www.rotodesign.com/gallery/japanese/

The Poetry of Subtitles page will have you in stitches. It lists a selection of actual Hong Kong movie subtitles like: 'I am damn unsatisfied to be killed in this way'; 'Same old rules: no eyes, no groin'; 'You always use violence. I should've ordered glutinous rice chicken'. The Japanese Snacks section is part of the same site and is worth a visit. The commentator has this to say about Lotte's Green Gum: 'That's more like it – a gum with the refreshing taste of PINE! Great, now my breath smells like a bathroom floor!' The Asparagus Biscuits sound delicious, too.

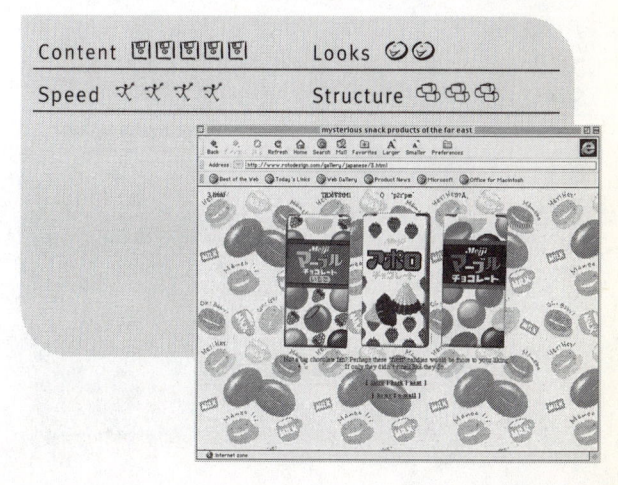

| Content | 🖼🖼🖼🖼 | Looks | ☺☺ |
| Speed | ✗ ✗ ✗ ✗ | Structure | 🌐🌐🌐 |

Distorted Barbie and the copyright scandal

http://www.users.interport.net/~napier/barbie/barbie.html

There are people out there who spend their time building web sites devoted to or bagging Barbie. Visit one and find out about Mattel's battle with Barbie fans online. Distorted Barbie, as it turns out, no longer features distorted versions of the blonde icon. The site's creator has masked the distorted images (apart from one of Kate Moss Barbie) and changed her name to $arbie or Barblie in a number of places to keep Mattel happy. The official Barbie site is at **www.barbie.com**.

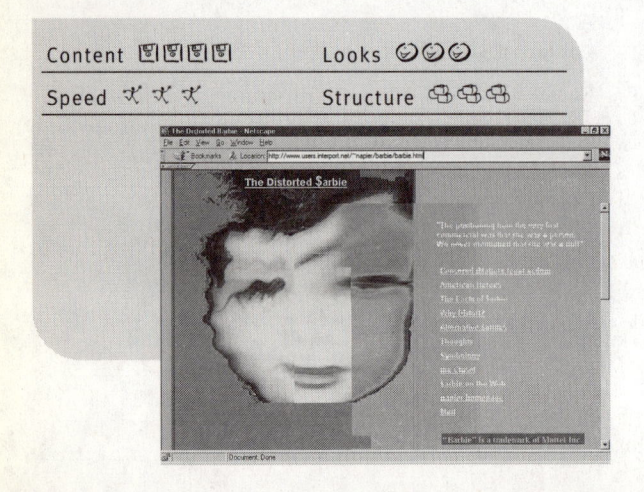

Content		Looks	
Speed		Structure	

Brain-hurting
http://www.theschwacorporation.com

The Schwa Corporation is a network of interrelated entities that is responsible for more than 37.15 per cent of new ideas being generated in the world. Hmmm. It's certainly responsible for one of the most incredible web sites around. The home page is so wide and so deep that scrolling through virtual star-filled skies seems endless. What Schwa really seems to be about is experimenting with graphics, Web navigation and your mind, using alien and conspiracy-theory themes. Very strange.

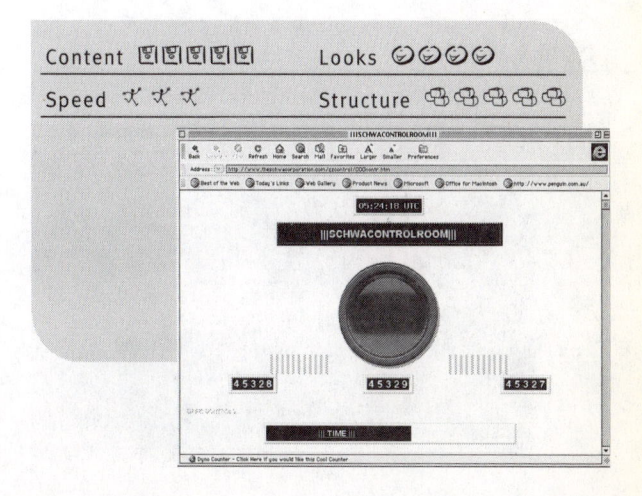

The infamous exploding whale
http://www.perp.com/whale/

'There's been a story floating around the Net for years about a beached whale that was blown up (exploded, not inflated) for lack of a better way to be rid of it.' Many people thought this story was an urban myth. As it turns out, a news crew viewed the historical event, and got the whole thing on tape. Luckily for us, someone with a lot of time on their hands was able to convert it to a handy digital format. It's true. Download in QuickTime and watch the blubber fly.

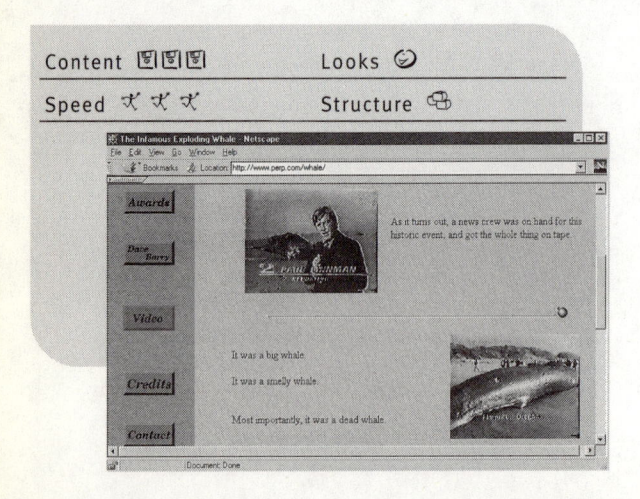

Content 🖻🖻🖻	Looks ☺
Speed ✄ ✄ ✄	Structure ♧

Lenin after death
http://www.gurlpages.com/spirit/linda.polley/lc.html

This 'online autobiography' opens with a greeting from its author: 'I am Vladimir Lenin. I am writing to you on a matter of most importance concerning NOT my life, or my earthly philosophy – these are well known; but concerning what happened to me AFTER my life.' Vlad reckons he spent 19 years after his death in blissful darkness before trying to communicate with other souls. The book was 'channelled' through a Portland-based 'spiritist', Gerald A. Polley. There is a link to the Polley home page, where you'll find more information on spiritism.

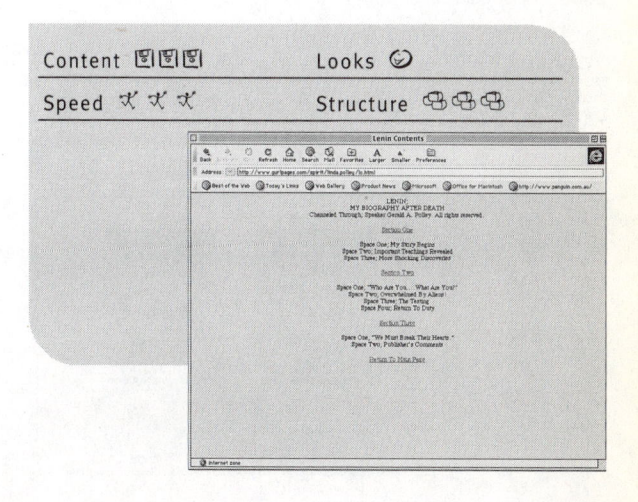

Content 🖺🖺🖺	Looks 😊
Speed ✈ ✈ ✈	Structure 🌐🌐🌐

173

Save Mr Toad's Wild Ride

http://www.savetoad.com

Heard about the campaign to stop Disneyworld from shutting down Mr Toad's Wild Ride? The site appeared the day after a newspaper report announced the possible closure. It promoted Save Toad T-shirts, postcards and downloadable flyers. Sadly, though, Toad's fun-park presence is to be replaced by Winnie-the-Pooh and friends. Mr Toad's last Wild Ride was on 7 September 1998: 'Join us that evening in front of Mr Toad's Wild Ride in the Magic Kingdom and watch [Disney chief Michael] Eisner gorge himself on Toad's blood in full view of the public. Metaphorically speaking, of course.'

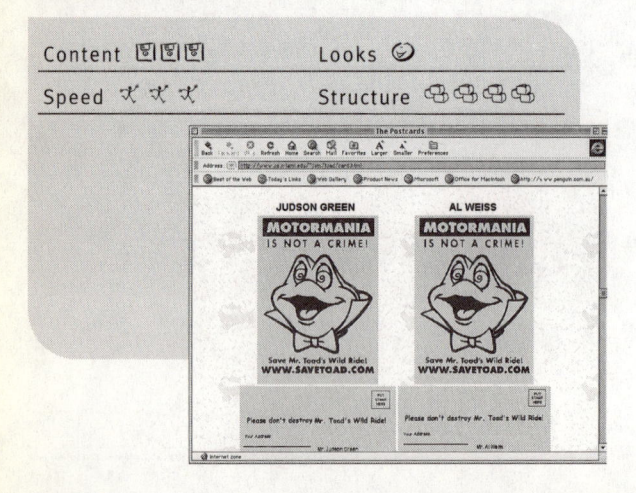

Content 🖻🖻🖻	Looks ☺
Speed � ✫ ✫	Structure 🐸🐸🐸🐸

Ransom, terrorism, space travel: are you covered?

http://www.steningsimpson.com.au

Stening Simpson is not your everyday suburban insurance company. It covers war; political risk; pre-launch, launch and in-orbit space travel; kidnap and ransom (including extortion, death and dismemberment); product tampering; sabotage and terrorism. SS employees track kidnap and ransom clients electronically and use the site to keep tabs on danger zones, safe houses and perilous situations.

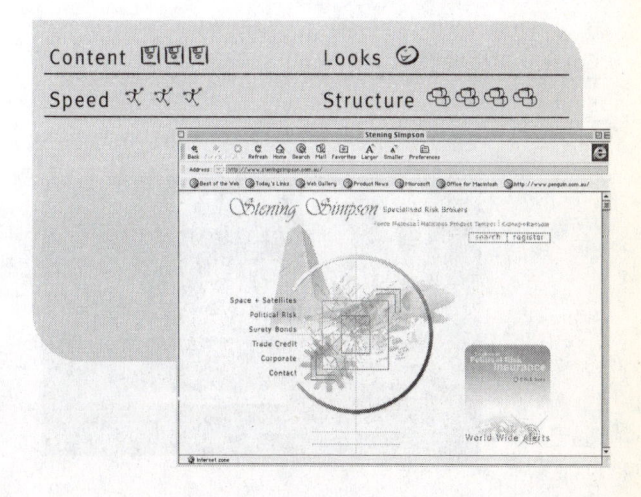

Content 🖻🖻🖻	Looks 😊
Speed ✗ ✗ ✗	Structure ⊕⊕⊕⊕

Evil Bert

http://fractalcow.com/bert/

Being a *Sesame Street* fan, I find it difficult to promote a web site that mocks all that is good about Cookie Monster, the Count, Oscar the Grouch and Mr Snufflehoweveryouspellit. But no Web surfer worth his or her salt can survive online without a cursory knowledge of the Bert is Evil site. Just remember, Bert isn't really like this. Parental guidance recommended.

Content 👿👿👿👿	Looks ☺☺☺
Speed ✈✈	Structure 🐌🐌🐌🐌

Sounds grave
http://www.findagrave.com

The fact that there is a site called Findagrave, that it truly lets you look up famous somebodies' graves (Elvis, for example) and view photos of them is weird. But not as weird as collecting dirt from the graves of noteworthy people, which is another favourite pastime of Jim Tipton (he's the berserk individual behind this site). It also allows you to search for final resting places by name, location or claim to fame and to view entries that include photographs, or choose from an array of Tipton's favourite morbid links.

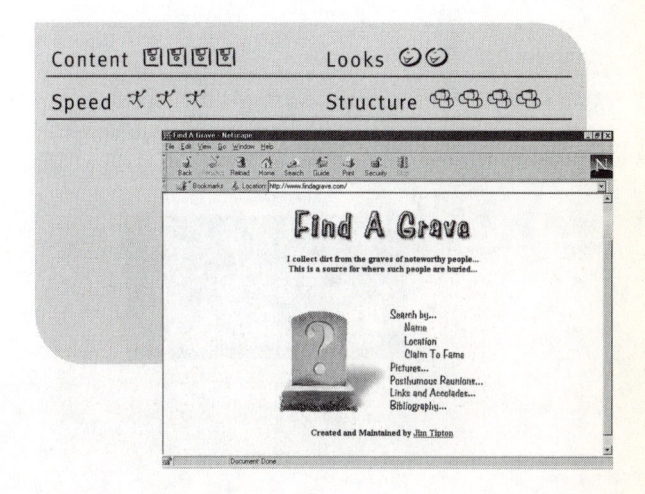

Content 🖥🖥🖥🖥   Looks 😊😊

Speed ✈ ✈ ✈   Structure 🐌🐌🐌🐌

Life of a pencil case

http://www.members.tripod.com/~leprikorn/

Sometimes the most entertaining bytes of the Web are not multi-million-dollar events. This cute site has been put together by a couple of Year 10 students from Trinity Grammar School in Sydney. It's about Leprikorn, who was not your average suburban pencil case. 'He lived in a small and dainty little semi-detached house in the inner-western suburbs of Sydney, Australia. He lived a hard life, at birth he suffered a severe case of pneumonia. The bout with the illness brought him to his current deformed state; small, green and fluffy. This is our dedication to the truly inspirational life of one fluffy, green pencil case.'

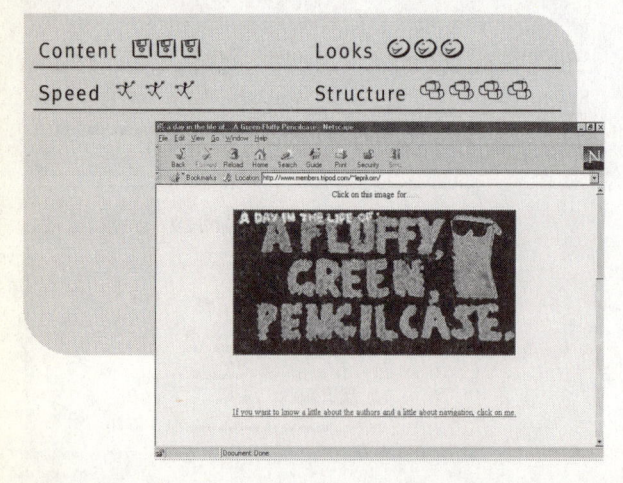

Content	📄📄📄	Looks	😊😊😊
Speed	✗ ✗ ✗	Structure	🐚🐚🐚🐚

City of the future
http://www.victorycities.com

Victory City sounds like a cross between the *Truman Show* set and the future-city in *The Fifth Element*. It's about creating sustainable and pleasurable places to live in the future, and the web site is stunning. In fact, the VC idea sounds OK until you get to the bit about food: 'In Victory City, everyone would eat in one of the large cafeterias rather than cooking for themselves. A large rotating serving counter called the Circl-Serv could feed approximately 16 333 people in only three and a half hours.' No more of my mother's cooking? Canteen food all day, every day? Life wouldn't be worth living.

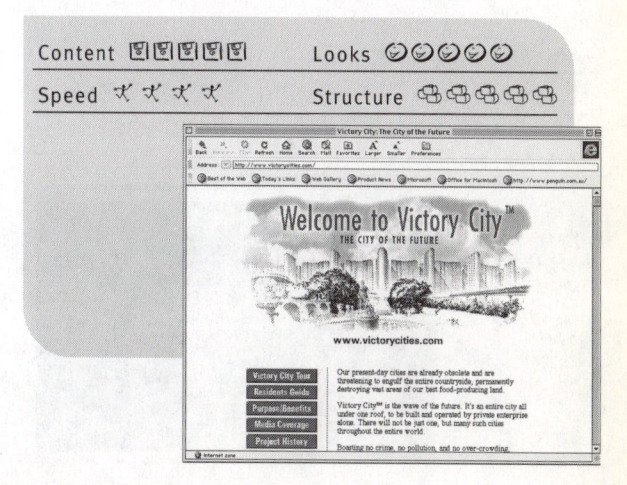

Content 🎬🎬🎬🎬🎬   Looks 😊😊😊😊😊

Speed ✗ ✗ ✗ ✗   Structure ⊖⊖⊖⊖⊖

Counting 'em down

http://www.deathclock.com

The Death Clock is one of those depressing-but-true reminders of just how short life is. After typing in your date of birth and your gender, wait while the clock calculates your date of death in Normal, Pessimistic or Sadistic mode. It then provides you with a ticker to count down the exact number of seconds till D-Day. I'd advise against Pessimism or Sadism – the normal date is soon enough. Look on the bright side, though. Being aware of how much or how little time you have should encourage you to make the most of every little bit of it.

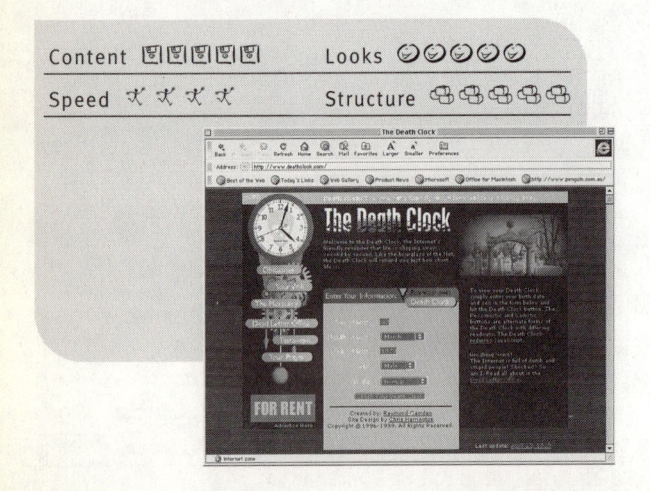

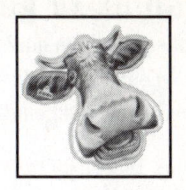

fourteen

Geek City

The Net is overrun with the sorts of people who talk about *Doctor Who* at parties, own every *Star Trek* movie on home video, and wish *Blake's Seven* had lived to a second series. Then there are those who yearn for a return to the DOS days, who spend most of their spare evenings playing Civ, are saving up for a detachable keyboard to plug into their PalmPilot, and wonder why their partners do not lust after their IBM ThinkPad. For every badly dressed geek, there's a closet nerd like me hoping no one will see through the 'I just do this for a living, after hours I'm your average groovy twentysomething' disguise. These sites will be useful and entertaining both to those who wear their geekiness on their sleeves and to those who hide it.

Guide to geek love

http://college.antioch.edu/~totally/geek.html
http://www.eecis.udel.edu/~masterma/GuideToGeekGirls.html
http://www.eecis.udel.edu/~masterma/glasses/

'Why Geek Dudes Rule: They are generally available; other women will tend not to steal them; they can fix things; your parents will love them; they're smart.' The entertaining and amusing Girl's Guide to Geek Guys offers this information, as well as useful tips for finding geeks – such as 'Geeks always wear software T-shirts'. Hell, it may even entice you to give up stylish, good-looking bastards for good.

If you're a bloke looking for a geekgirl, try the second site, which was created in response to the first. It's more of an essay, explaining how to attract and keep a geekgirl.

Girls who need to know they're not alone in their geekiness should visit Guide to GeekGirls' sister site, Girls Who Wear Glasses: 'One of the stereotypes that irks me the most is the story where the geek girl has to take off her glasses, undo her ponytail, and dress like everyone else before a guy will take notice. What results is not a magical transformation, but someone in ill-fitting borrowed clothes whose hair keeps falling in her face and who bumps into things.'

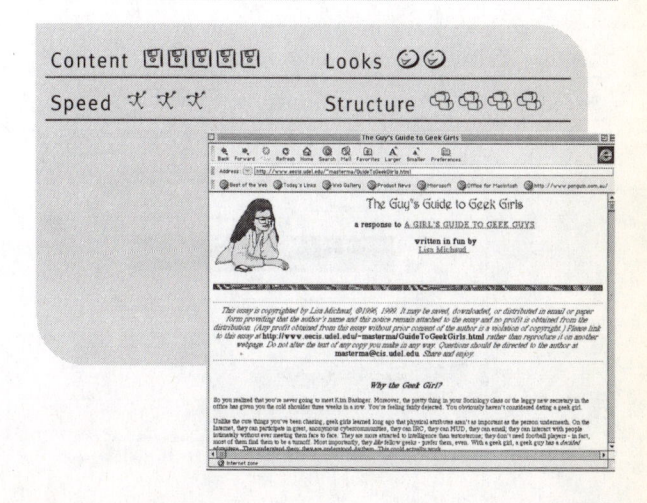

Content 📖📖📖📖📖   Looks 😊😊

Speed ✈ ✈ ✈   Structure 🏠🏠🏠🏠

Search voyeur

http://voyeur.mckinley.com/cgi-bin/voyeur.cgi

Have you ever thought that people might be watching you surf? This site shows you 12 randomly selected real-time searches that are taking place at the Magellan search engine, updated every 15 seconds. Here's a random sample: Colombian drug cartels, fetish hair, embroidery, where can I tip cows, smack my bitch up, spicegirl. Fascinating. If you see a search topic that sounds interesting, click on it to see what Magellan has come up with.

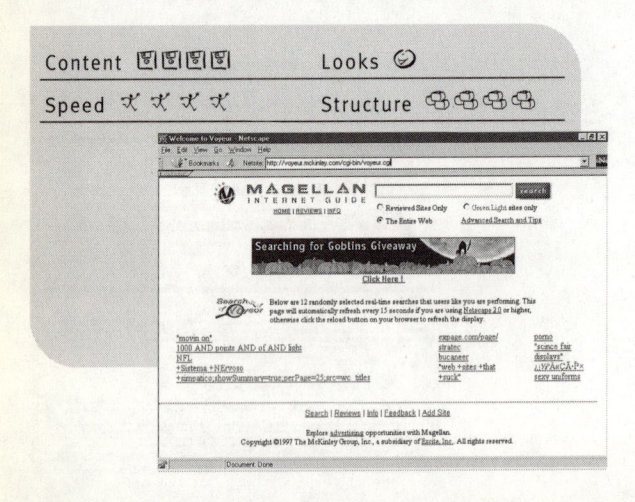

Content	📖📖📖📖	Looks	☺
Speed	✈ ✈ ✈ ✈	Structure	🌐🌐🌐🌐

Soccer robotics

http://www.robocup.v.kinotrope.co.jp/02.html

The Robot World Cup Initiative seems to be a combination of a bunch of soccer and robotics nuts meeting for the fun of it and a legitimate piece of scientific research. It's deadly serious, though, when it says: 'By mid-21st century, a team of fully autonomous humanoid robot soccer players shall win the soccer game, comply with the official rules of the FIFA, against the winner of the most recent World Cup.' It reckons the fact that Deep Blue was able to beat the world champion at chess within 50 years of the invention of the digital computer shows that its dream is not as far-fetched as it may seem.

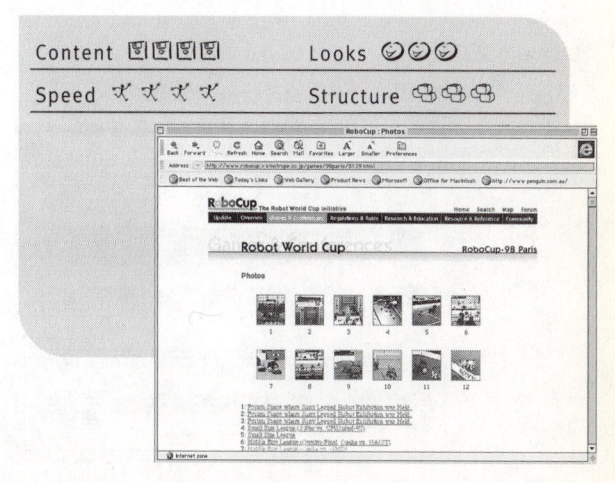

Content 🖳🖳🖳🖳   Looks ☺☺☺

Speed ✗ ✗ ✗ ✗   Structure 🗜🗜🗜

The astrology of an operating system
http://www.besys.net.au/win95.html

For a quick laugh, check out 'If Microsoft Win95 was ruled by . . .'. If it's Aries, it will tell you how brilliant it is at every opportunity and even pop up with message windows such as 'Don't you think I'm wonderful?' while you are working. (The options are yes or yes.) On the other hand, if Win95 was ruled by Libra you could at least 'bet your desktop will never look messy or misaligned – even if it did sweet-talk the other software into doing the cleaning'.

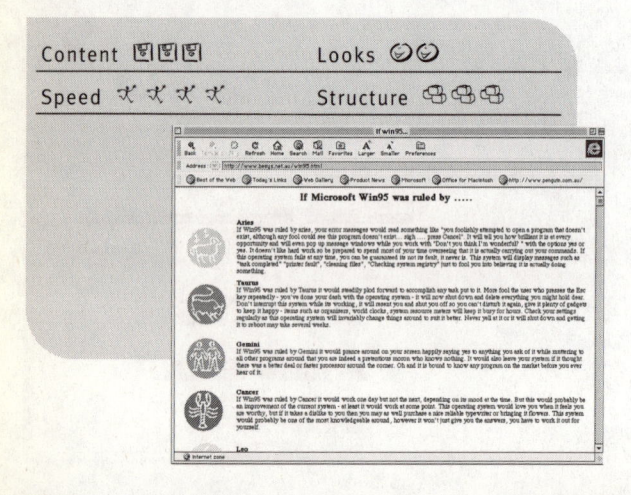

Content 📖📖📖	Looks 😊😊
Speed ✈✈✈✈	Structure 🌐🌐🌐

Mysterious Mac magic

http://www.yaromat.com/macos/

This site is very groovy. I hesitate to tell you too much about it because I don't want to spoil the surprise. Here's a clue, though: 'Please write me about this fake Macintosh.' And another one: 'Unfortunately Windows remains on your hard disk.' Watch it convert your PC into a Mac before your eyes, with clever HTML that makes the page work just the way the Mac OS would have if that's what it really was, which it isn't if it's not one to begin with . . . but don't let that confuse you. Click on the trash can to see the Windows logo sitting in a bin. Go there.

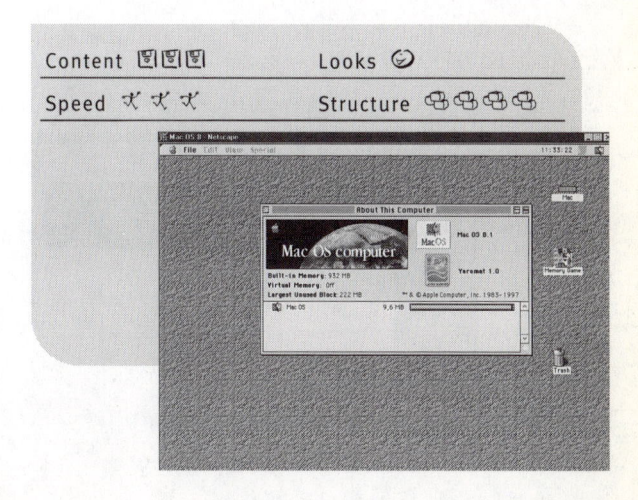

Content 🖻🖻🖻   Looks ☺
Speed �† ✝ ✝   Structure ♘♘♘♘

The electric monk

http://www.electricmonk.com

Electric Monk is one of the coolest Web gadgets around. The search tool takes its name from a Douglas Adams novel, *Dirk Gently's Holistic Detective Agency*. It lets you type in real questions which it 'understands'. So you can ask 'How do I make pancakes?' or 'What time is it in Boston?' and it will analyse the question, formulate a complex boolean query, send that to a back-end search engine such as Altavista, and give you the results. Not that the results are necessarily what you're looking for, but it's a nice idea.

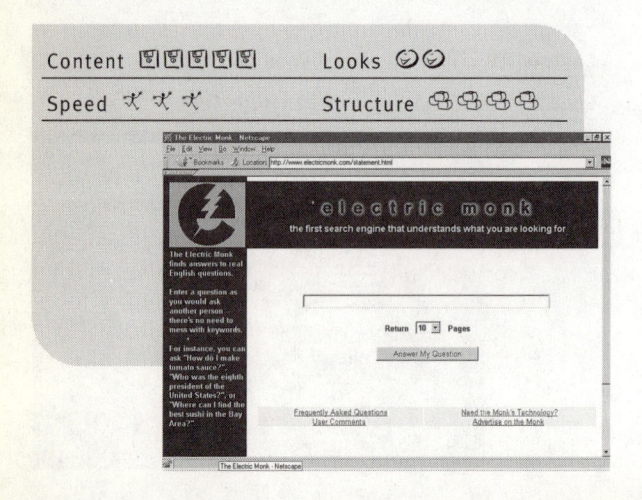

Content 🖳🖳🖳🖳🖳	Looks ☺☺
Speed ✈ ✈ ✈	Structure 🐌🐌🐌🐌

Message me on my mobile
http://www.mtnsms.com

This is way cool – a site that allows you to send text messages of up to 150 characters to any mobile phone, although the service is currently disabled for Optus mobiles. It's better than ringing and speaking to your most wanted because it's free, and we find they tend to call back when they get the message anyway.

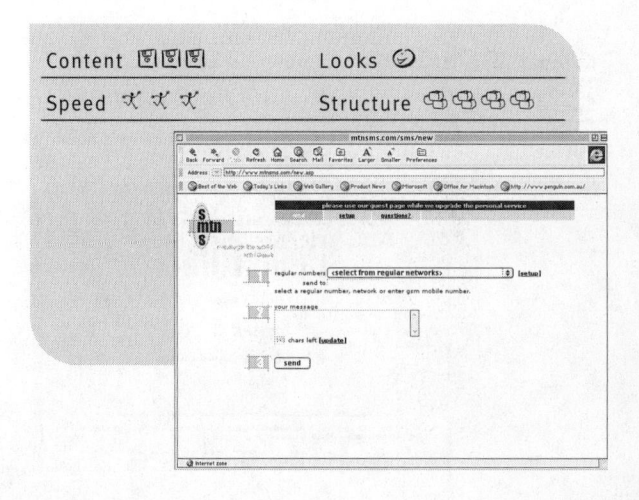

Content 📖📖📖	Looks ☺
Speed ✗ ✗ ✗	Structure 🌀🌀🌀🌀

Cool palm computing
http://web.one.net.au/~coolcol

The Australian and New Zealand Palm Pilot home page is maintained by a group called Cool Col Productions. OK, so it's really just a nice bloke called Colin Merrilees who's into Palm Pilots. His site is not linked to the official Palm people in any way besides html – it's strictly a hobby site for Col. Which is not to say it's not really, really handy. There are Palm Pilot links, downloads, frequently asked questions, news, help for technical problems and a contact list you can join.

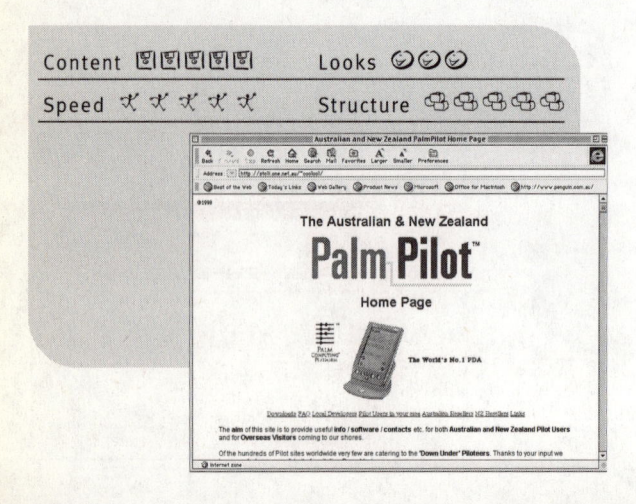

Content ☺☺☺☺☺   Looks ☺☺☺
Speed ✗ ✗ ✗ ✗ ✗   Structure ♨♨♨♨

Flight sim heaven

http://www.migman.com.au

MiGMan says his site is the Web's biggest (there are 800 pages) devoted to combat flight sims and how to fly them. The Australian site's Flight Sim Museum traces the genre from its beginnings in 1980 in pictures, sound and animation. It sits alongside information on F-111s in Australia; sim hardware, videos and air combat fiction; maps; newsgroups; and guides to flying sims.

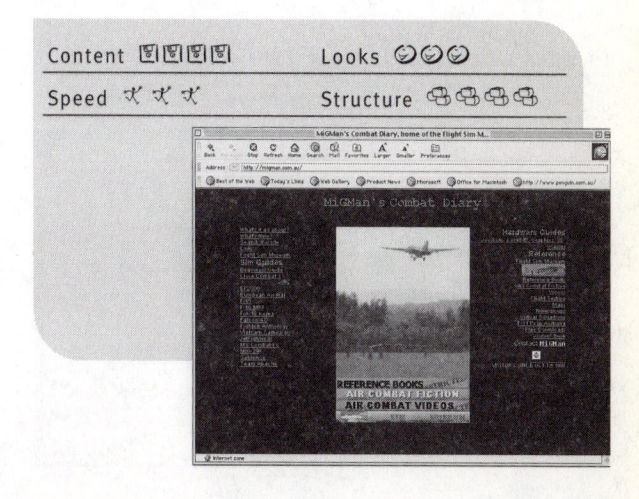

Content 🖳🖳🖳🖳   Looks ☺☺☺

Speed ✈ ✈ ✈   Structure 🐢🐢🐢🐢

Mind your sites

http://netmind.com/

Charles Darwin said, 'It is not the strongest of the species that survive, nor the most intelligent, but the one most responsive to change.' Five million Internet users can't be wrong. They're regulars at NetMind, a site that allows you to track changes at your favourite sites without constant return visits. Sign up to be alerted to changes to text, numbers, images, forms, links and keywords. The information is sent via email or stored at Minder Central, a Web-based list of everything Mind-it tracks for you.

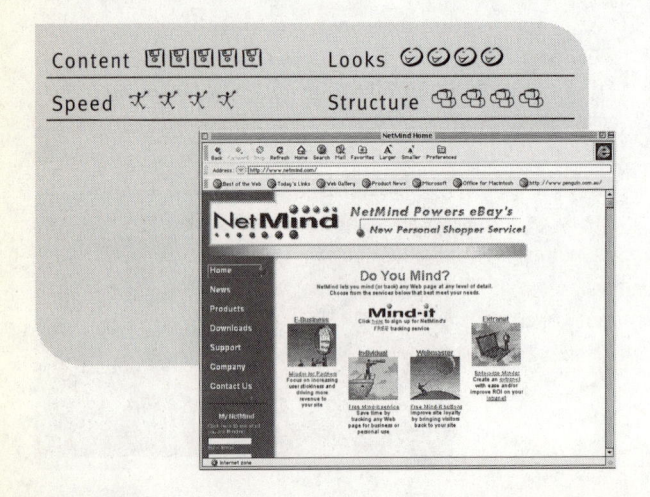

Content	🖼🖼🖼🖼	Looks	😊😊😊😊
Speed	✈✈✈✈	Structure	🌐🌐🌐🌐

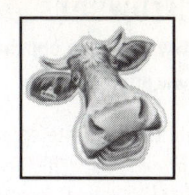

fifteen

Bare Essentials

Think of this section as the appendix. You won't have been able to enjoy any of the sites mentioned in this book without knowing about browsers and search engines. Taking a look at the Web charts will give you a context for the sites you've read about here, and an idea of what everyone else who's busy surfing is looking at. Sites like the online White Pages, ICQ and the dictionary will save you so much time and hassle, you'll wonder how you ever coped without them. Bookmark them.

Browsers

http://www.netscape.com.au
http://www.microsoft.com

Alongside the requisite computer, modem, phone line, Internet service provider, specific access phone number and password, your choice of a Web browser – probably one of the big two, Netscape Navigator or Microsoft Internet Explorer (IE) – is your key to the online world. Once you type or paste in a Web address, your browser searches the Net and asks the relevant Web server (which is just a computer somewhere else in the world, also connected to the Net, and housing the site you want to see) for the page you're after. The browser collects the requested HTML file and any images or multimedia files it refers to and displays them on your terminal.

It's worth keeping your browser up to date because the latest versions often include functionality only available through plug-ins for earlier versions. Download the current version from one of the addresses above. If you're not sure how to download software from the Net, visit the *Sydney Morning Herald*'s Icon web site at **www.smh.com.au/icon/**, then click through to the Net 101 Downloading section. Beware, downloading a browser can take a while. Don't sit and watch. Take a tea break.

Once you have your browser organised, learn to use your bookmarks (known as favourites in IE). They'll save you lots of time down the track. Icon has a tutorial on them too. Also make sure you check your browser settings, options or preferences.

That's where you can make sure that your home or start page is one you want to come back to every time you sign on, like your favourite news or sports site, rather than your boring old ISP site or the Microsoft site. Also check that the colours, fonts and other options are set appropriately (it can make a big difference to the way some sites look).

Finally, be aware of caching. This means that if you've looked at a page recently, your browser may have kept a copy of it (in cache) to make it quicker to pull down in the future. To make sure you're seeing the latest version, hold down the shift key and click on the reload (Navigator) or refresh (IE) button.

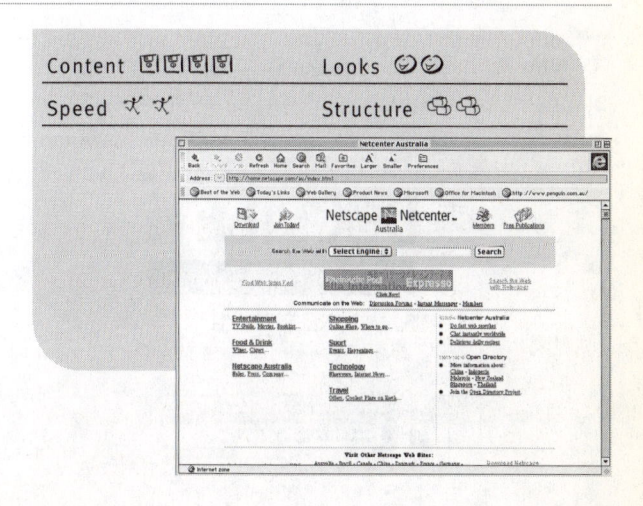

Content 📧📧📧📧   Looks 😊😊

Speed ✗ ✗   Structure 🔗🔗

Search engines and Web directories

http://www.dogpile.com
http://www.yahoo.com.au

By now you have some idea of the information available on the Web, so you're ready to go out and hunt down your own favourite useful or wacky sites. Dogpile is great if you want the most comprehensive listing of sites available on a particular topic. It sifts through a dozen or so search engines, then lists all of their findings. If you're in a hurry, Yahoo is a better bet.

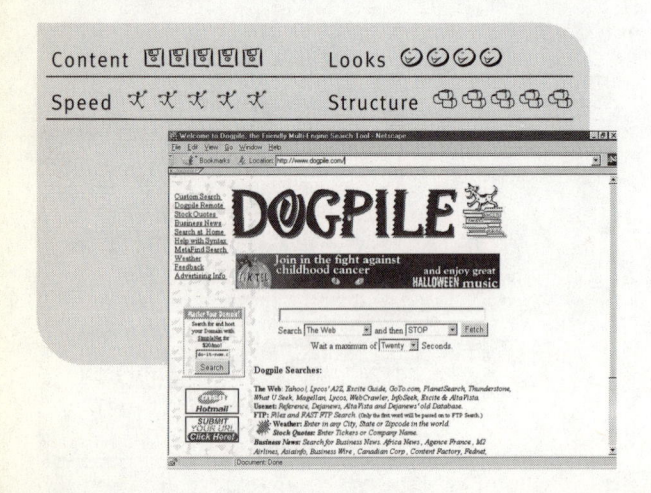

Content 👿👿👿👿👿   Looks 😊😊😊😊
Speed 🐾🐾🐾🐾🐾   Structure 🐶🐶🐶🐶🐶

Plug-ins
http://www.macromedia.com/shockwave/download/
http://www.realplayer.com

A plug-in is an accessory that enhances your browser's capabilities. The number of sites you'll visit that require plug-ins will drive you mad early on, but once you've installed the main ones, you can forget all about them and enjoy the ride. Sites that require them will let you know, and direct you to other sites to download them. Shockwave lets you play games and use interactive sections of sites developed using that technology, while RealPlayer is a must for most of the video and lots of the audio you'll find online.

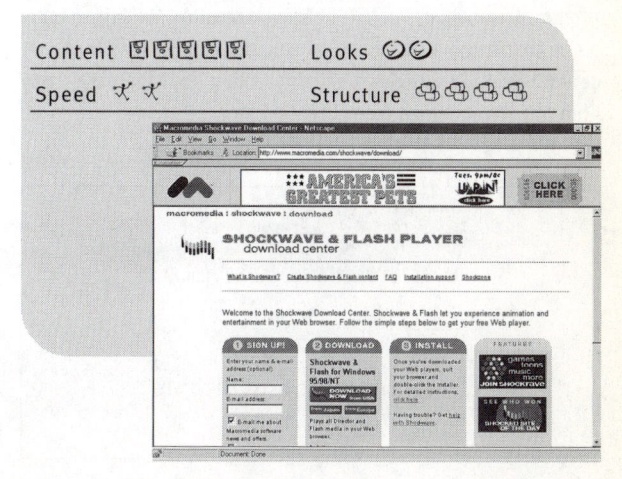

Content 🗹🗹🗹🗹 Looks ☺☺

Speed ✈ ✈ Structure 🐢🐢🐢🐢

Newsgroups and mailing lists

http://www.deja.com
http://www.neosoft.com/internet/paml/

Newsgroups and Usenet date back to the Internet's pre-Web text-only days. They're online discussion groups, and Deja News provides a Web interface so that anyone can easily read, search, participate in and subscribe to more than 80 000 of them. It's a brilliant way of finding people with similar interests, getting answers to tricky questions, and generally passing the time. Which was what I was doing when I looked up British TV program *This Life* and instead found a posting on the **rec.arts.sf.starwars.misc** forum entitled 'Re: Yoda's Sex Life'. Hmmm. Meanwhile, PAML (Publicity Accessible Mailing Lists) is a site that archives information on more mailing lists than you could ever have imagined existing – how about joining Carlo Chiopris's Italian yoga email list? Perhaps not.

No screen grab available
at this time

Web events

http://www.onnow.com

There are so many live events happening every minute online that you almost need a full-time researcher to sift through and find the ones that are worth tuning in for. Fortunately, On Now is a site that does just that. Although it caters to the US market, its Top Picks section often includes chats with TV stars, musicians or politicians or live Webcasts of events like the Oscars, Tibetan Freedom Concert or Sydney's own Mardi Gras.

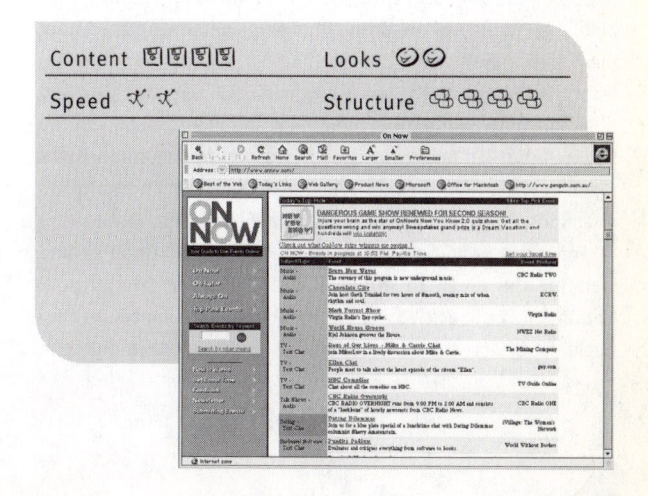

Content ☺☺☺☺   Looks ☺☺
Speed ✓ ✓   Structure ☺☺☺☺

Web-based email, ICQ and IRC

http://www.hotmail.com
http://www.start.com.au
http://www.yahoo.com.au
http://www.icq.com

Try free, Web-based email that you can access from any computer connected to the Web anywhere in the world. Invent a ridiculous address for yourself, like the revolting individual (we love you apart from your email address, Andrew) who travels cyberspace as burpfartsnot@hotmail.com, or entirely invented personas (I use Amelia, who emails all kinds of people charper@access.fairfax.com.au couldn't possibly). It's also a good way of ensuring your employers don't read your mail, and there's every chance they do just that. (At the very least the IT department has a giggle at your personal life every now and then.) Hotmail is the oldest and most popular of the services, but it's now owned by Microsoft, so some anti-Gates types might prefer to choose Australia's Start, which also offers a reminder service for birthdays and anniversaries.

For those of you who want to chat now rather than sit and wait for the email to arrive, ICQ and IRC are two of your options. ICQ ('I seek you') is like instantaneous email. As they put it: 'ICQ lets you find your friends and associates online in real time. You can create a contact List containing only people you want to have there, you can send them messages, chat with them, send files, configure ICQ to work with external applications and more.'

IRC is a pre-Web technology that allows you to chat in real time to people you know, and people you don't. Take an IRC tutorial in the Net 101 section at **www.smh.com.au/icon**.

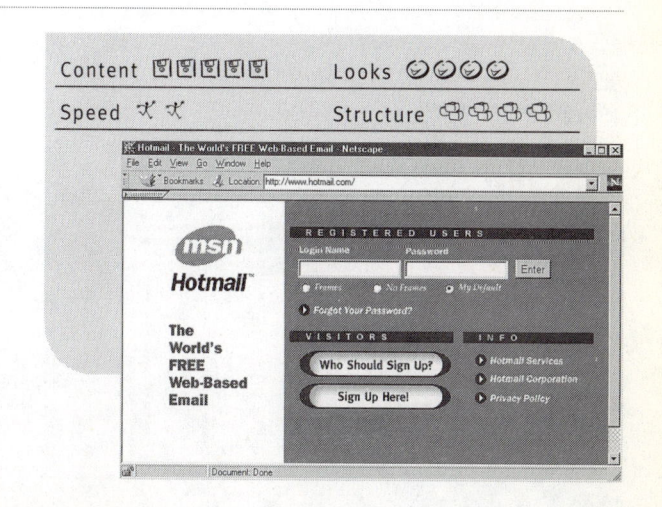

Content 🖫🖫🖫🖫🖫   Looks ☺☺☺☺

Speed ✵ ✵   Structure ⌬⌬⌬⌬

Web charts: who's hot

http://www.mpx.com.au/~ianw/
http://www.100hot.com
http://www.100hot.com/world/australia/au/

Some charts are better than others. I prefer listening to tracks that feature in Triple J's Hottest 100 than to those topping Billboard's list, for example. But whether they tell you what people are listening to on CD, watching at the movies or on television, buying at the bookshop or pointing their Web browsers at, the charts give you an insight into our culture as it is right here and now.

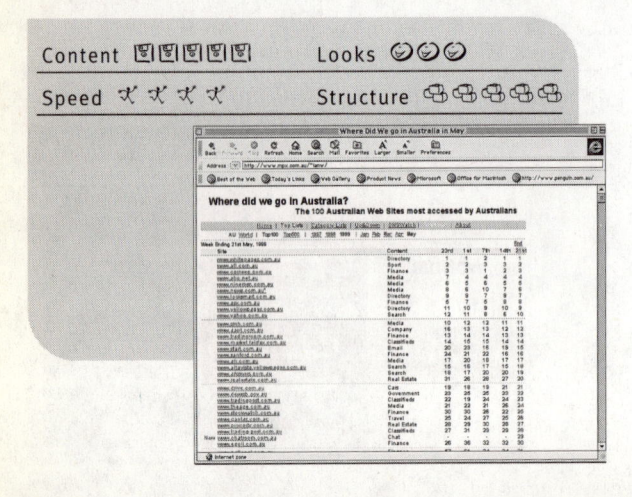

Content 🗒️🗒️🗒️🗒️🗒️ Looks ☺☺☺

Speed � ✍ ✍ ✍ Structure 🐟🐟🐟🐟🐟

Your own Web space

http://www.visto.com

Visit Visto, sign up for free, and post your family photos or latest artworks on your own little piece of their server. It's easy. This site has been around for a couple of years, so they've had time to simplify the process. And once your photos and files are up there, you can pass your password and username on to anyone you think would care to see your images and information.

Content 🖺🖺🖺🖺
Looks ☺☺☺☺
Speed ✗ ✗ ✗ ✗
Structure 🗘🗘🗘🗘🗘

Plain-speaking legal eagles
http://www.law4u.com.au

Nothing beats plain English. Choose from a growing list of fact sheets, including pages on child support, divorce, buying and selling a house, wills and driving offences. That's the serious stuff. The fun bit, Law in the Lounge, features reviews of books, films and TV programs with legal themes. The Footy Law section sets out the Aussie Rules rules. A regular column called The Law Spot explains current legal affairs in simple terms, from Bill Gates v. the US Department of Justice to the dating agency that thought it was fair to tell a blind woman she couldn't join. Sign up to receive email notification of updates.

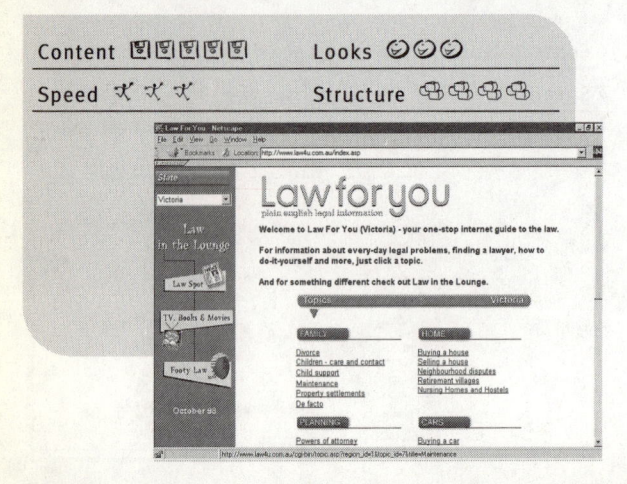

Content	📖📖📖📖📖	Looks	☺☺☺
Speed	✈✈✈	Structure	🐌🐌🐌🐌

Can't turn the clock back, baby

http://www.dstc.qut.edu.au/DST/marg/daylight.html

Turning clocks backwards and forwards in the early hours of a Sunday morning has become a part of life for most of us twice a year because of daylight saving. This site lists which Australian states change times and when, provides a link to software that corrects daylight saving for Windows 95 in Sydney and Melbourne, and gives a short history of Australian standard time. And did you know that in 1986, a day did not equal 24 hours but 24.00000034 hours? Well, now you do.

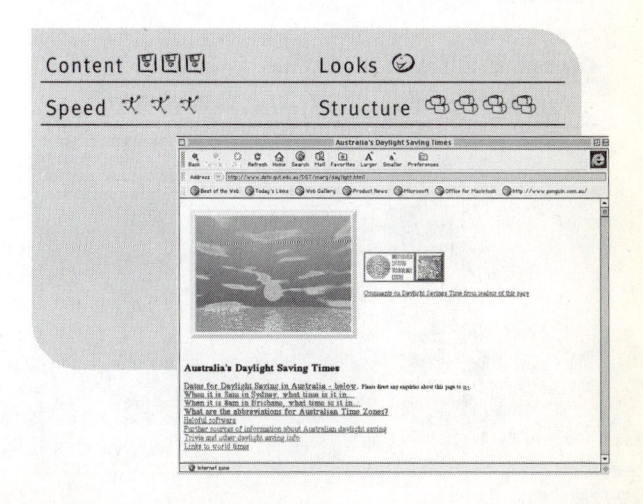

Content 📖📖📖	Looks 😊
Speed ✄ ✄ ✄	Structure 🌐🌐🌐🌐

Travel

http://www.lonelyplanet.com
http://www.travel.com.au

Save time and money by planning your next travel experience online. Find out the best time to visit, where to stay, how to get around once you're there, what it'll cost and what to see. Then book it all online. Australian guidebook specialist Lonely Planet's site provides maps, photos, links, travel writing, bulletin boards, health information and travellers' reports. **Travel.com.au** features booking facilities for airfares, packages, accommodation and car rental.

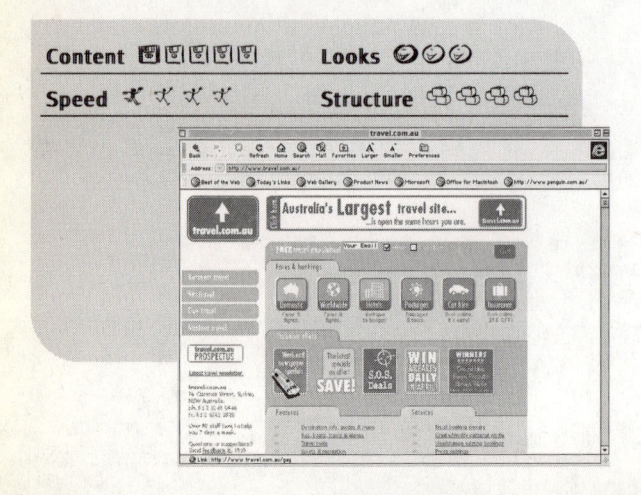

Content	🖺🖺🖺🖺	Looks	😊😊😊
Speed	✈✈✈✈	Structure	🏛🏛🏛🏛

Government online

http://www.peo.gov.au
http://www.fed.gov.au
http://www.acn.net.au

The Parliamentary Education Office web site has virtual tours of Parliament House that are better than being there (plus you don't have to deal directly with the politicians). Grown-ups will find the Australian Commonwealth Government Entry Point a useful site to bookmark. It provides links to and information on every government department and agency in the country. Australia's Cultural Network points out cultural organisations, web sites, resources, news and events.

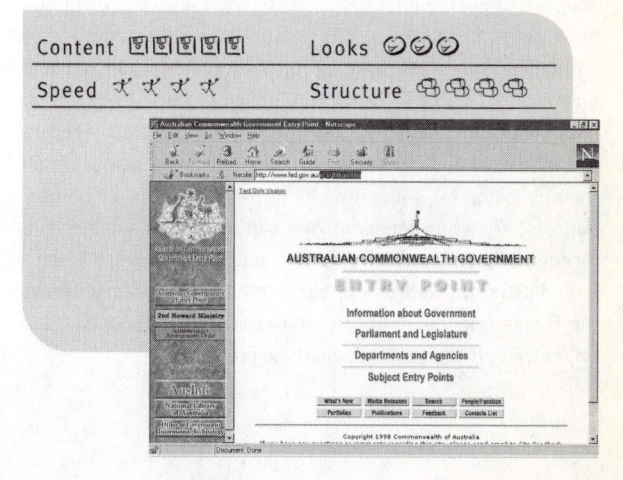

Content 👁👁👁👁👁 Looks 😊😊😊
Speed ✗ ✗ ✗ ✗ Structure 🕸🕸🕸🕸

Really, really useful sites

http://www.dictionary.com
http://www.thesaurus.com
http://www.whitepages.com.au
http://www.yellowpages.com.au
http://www.bom.gov.au
http://www.calculator.com
http://www.xe.net/currency/
http://www.hilink.com.au/00/times/
http://www.whowhere.com
http://www.legioncabs.com.au/bookings.html

You need never search for a dictionary, thesaurus or phone book again, because you can find phone numbers, synonyms and definitions online. Waiting for the weather report to come on the radio? Check it now at the Bureau of Meteorology's web site. Lost your calculator? Use the one on the Web. Need to convert times and currencies to work out travel plans? It's all there. Looking for a long-lost friend who might have an email address? Try **whowhere.com**. You can also book a cab online through Legion's web site, check your bank balance if your bank has introduced online banking and book your business trip through Qantas or Ansett online. If it can possibly be done on the Web, it can probably be done on the Web.

My pick for Australia's most useful web site is **www.whitepages.com.au**. Postcodes at your fingertips; world time and dialling codes; every listed phone number in the country – now that's handy. It also provides a link to Whereis, which is a street atlas covering major urban areas of Australia. Type in an address and watch as the appropriate piece of cyberUBD appears. Zoom in and out, too. Wow.

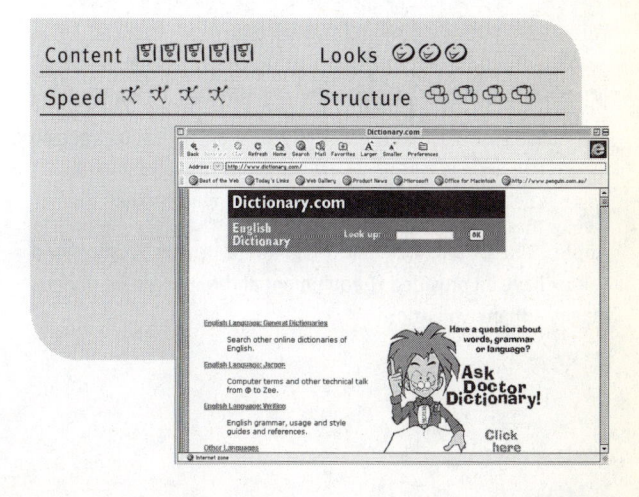

Content 🖳🖳🖳🖳   Looks 😊😊😊

Speed ✈ ✈ ✈ ✈   Structure 🕮🕮🕮🕮

Acknowledgements

The trouble with little books is that there isn't room to thank everyone. And in the case of this little book, almost every site was created by, and in many cases pointed out by, someone who deserves a special thank-you. So thanks. You know who you are.

Thanks to Jon Casimir, Tony Sarno and Lynne Whiley at the *Sydney Morning Herald*, where many of these site reviews first appeared.

At Penguin, specific thanks go to Julie Gibbs for embracing the idea and Laurie Critchley, Lisa Mills, Melissa Fraser, Foong Ling Kong and Katie Purvis for making it work.

To my friends, thanks for leaving me alone when I needed to write, but being there when I needed you.

Most of all I'd like to thank David, Diana, Sophie and Nick, for encouraging and supporting me through this and other trials of the late 1900s.

P.S.

Apple, Sirius, IBM, Ozemail, Magnadata, Angus Kidman and Fairfax have all provided IT equipment and Net access at various stages – thank you, too.

Credits

Chapter 1 Games and Other Time Wasters
Finger twister: Spin, London (www.spin.co.uk)
Your special subject is: Kipper Communications

Chapter 2 Media
American media: copyright © 1998 The New York Times Company. Reprinted by permission.
Urban films: Urban Cinefile, Australia's online movie magazine; winner, Best Arts & Entertainment Site, *Aust Fin Review*/Telstra 1998 Internet Awards

Chapter 3 Sporty Stuff
Goal attack: Netball Australia – capturing sport, health and fun
Squash vital people: courtesy of the International Squash Federation
Try these: Paul Brand
Snow sports: copyright © 1996, 1997, 1998 or 1999 Leisurenet Australia Pty Ltd
Hot-air ballooning history: Grahame Wilson, Lane Cove, Sydney

Chapter 4 Music
Massive: illustration courtesy of Virgin Records
Music information overload: copyright © 1995–99 iMusic Inc.
Music media: from IMMEDIA! home of the Australasian Music Industry Directory, Australian Sports Industry Directory and In Music & Media online weekly music magazine

Chapter 5 Fans and Anti-fans
The Amazing SPAM Homepage: appears courtesy of its creator, Polly Esther Fabrique (March Rosenbluth)
Pride and prejudice: original art at the Republic of Pemberley by Hilary Talbot, Canberra

Chapter 6 Up Close and Personal
Therapeutic thoughts: Pipsqueak Productions
Sex and the single Aussie: the Durex web site was created by AKQA New Media (www.akqa.com)

Risky questions: copyright reserved by Tripod, a Lycos company
The free cybermarriage site: thanks to Kanga and all the lovers on the Internet who made this page possible
I had sex with Clinton: copyright © DreaMasters, Inc.
Love calculator: copyright © Thijs Kinkhorst and Matthijs Sypkens Smit

Chapter 7 Shopping
Feral Cheryl: Feral Cheryl created by Lee Duncan, web design Geoff Hill, artwork Jenny Hull

Chapter 8 Being There
World Webcams: created and maintained by Steve Fuchs
Hip and groovy art: the Museum of Contemporary Art's web site has been designed and built by MCA's Online Media Partner – Spike
Long macchiato: Damn Fine Coffee
Homesick Australians abroad: Australians Abroad is operated and edited by Richard Rankin and Kate Juliff

Chapter 9 Good Causes
Human rights: Amnesty International Australia acknowledges Webaid (Spike, Compaq, Microsoft and Ozemail) for support of the site
Here comes the Republic: thanks to the Australian Republican Movement
A new flag: Ausflag Ltd

Chapter 10 Kids and School
Email penpals: a free site provided by Topnet Internet – Specialists in Web Sites for Small Business
Online gardening: copyright © 1999, Nickelodeon. All rights reserved.
Race across time: AT&T Virtual Classroom, Powerhouse Museum
Fressshhhhh fruit: Sydney Markets Limited
Languages of the world: reproduced by permission of the Summer Institute of Linguistics, Inc.

Chapter 11 DIY
Dance hall dazzlers: Ballroomdancers.com is designed and operated by Jonathan Atkinson and Melissa Winogrand of Los Angeles, California

Green thumbs: Global Garden is designed and published by Global Garden Pty Ltd
Personal trainer: provided with the permission of BFIT on the Net
Quit smoking: another Wow on the Web by Crystal Sky Productions at http://www.WowMe.com
Home handyperson: Jerry Alonzy, owner and webmaster, The Natural Handyman

Chapter 12 Awards
Australian Internet Awards: courtesy of *The Australian Financial Review/Telstra Australian Internet Awards*
Razzies: David Kalin and DK Digital Media – creators and webmasters
Webbies: web site created by vivid studios and The Webby Awards
Time 100 poll: copyright © 1999 Time Inc. New Media. All rights reserved. Reproduction in whole or in part without permission is prohibited. Pathfinder is a registered trademark of Time Inc. New Media.
Darwin Awards: copyright © 1998–99 www.DarwinAwards.com

Chapter 13 Truly Weird
Brain-hurting: copyright © Schwa, Inc.
Lenin after death: Speaker Gerald A. Polley, Spiritist Publications
Save Mr Toad's Wild Ride: special thanks to jef moskot
Life of a pencil case: Matthew Leaver and Patrick Santamaria

Chapter 14 Geek City
Soccer robotics: copyright © 1999, The RoboCup Federation

Chapter 15 Bare Essentials
Web events: OnNow – The Internet's Leading Guide to Live Online Events
Plain-speaking legal eagles: Weblink (web designer)
Can't turn the clock back, baby: this page was created by Margaret Turner, Principal Consultant, Distributed Systems Technology Centre

Index

Aboriginal Australia 127, 145
Adams, Jessica 86
animals 113, 123;
  see also dogs
Animorphs 140
Antarctica 114
art 109, 117
astrology 25, 86, 186
Austen, Jane 73
Australian Broadcasting
  Corporation 24–5
Australian Rules football 45
Australian War Memorial 112
Australians abroad 115
awards 157
  Australian Internet Awards
    158
  Bobbies 161
  Darwin Awards 164
  Razzies 160
  Schools Web Challenge 159
  Time Person of the
    Century 163
  Webbies 162

ballooning 54
Barbie 91, 170
basketball 47
boats 92

bookmarks 194
books 73, 96–7
Bragg, Billy 74
browsers 194–5
bubble wrap 21

caching 195
charities 119–26
  Amnesty International 126
  Australian Conservation
    Foundation 122
  Community Aid Abroad 124
  Guide Dog Association 121
  Reach Out 120
  RSPCA 123
  Salvation Army 125
chocolates 82
Clinton, Bill 17, 24, 81
coffee 110
conservation 122
cooking 154
cricket 40–1
croquet 52

dancing 149
dancing baby 61
daylight saving 205
death 84, 177, 180
Dinnigan, Collette 90

dinosaurs 141
Discovery Channel 113
Disney 139, 174
dogs 18, 94, 121

email 200
exercise 151

FBI 142
Feral Cheryl 91
flags 129
flight simulators 191
flowers 100
fruit 103, 143

games
  air hockey 12
  Blackjack 8
  crosswords 9
  finger twister 6
  hackey sack 11
  Mastermind 10
  Pacman 7
  pool 5
  Race Across Time 136
  Snoot 19
  Superfro 20
gardening 133, 150
Gates, Bill 67
golf 51
Goosebumps 140

government 207
graves 177

history 136
hockey 38
home repairs 155
horse racing 50
human rights 126

ICQ 200–1
insurance 175
IRC 200–1

Kahootz 137
Keating, Paul 75
kids, web sites for 130, 132–3,
  135–41, 143–4
Knievel, Evel 79

languages 16, 146
laws 204
Lenin, Vladimir 173
love 80, 85, 87, 182–3

mailing lists 198
maps 107
Mardi Gras 111
marriage 80, 88
McGauchey, Ingrid 114
media
  Australian Broadcasting
    Corporation 24–5

Australian, The 25
British Broadcasting
  Corporation 26
CNET 28
Geekgirl 32
Immedia 62
LOUD 33
New York Times, The 27
Ninemsn 25
Onion, The 28–9
Salon 29
Sydney Morning Herald, The 24–5
Triple J 31
urban cinefile 30
Wired 28
millennium 116
Minogue, Dannii 68
mobile phones 189
Monty Python 70–1
movies 13–14, 30, 70, 93, 160
MP3 62
Museum of Contemporary Art 109
music 31, 55–64, 69, 74, 98, 152

names 167
netball 46
news 24–9
newsgroups 198

number plates 166

Oasis 66
Olympic Games 36–7
origami 148

palm computers 190
parents 82–3
penpals 132
plug-ins 197
politics 75, 126, 128
polls 31, 157, 163
Pride and Prejudice 73

radio 13, 63
religion 168
Rugby League 44
Rugby Union 43

Schwa Corporation 171
science 25, 113, 118, 135
search engines 196
Sesame Street 176
sex 78, 81
shopping 89–103
skiing 53
smoking 153
soccer 42, 185
South Park 72, 163
Spam 71
Spice Girls 69

216

sport
  US web sites 36
  Australian Sports Commission 36
  see also individual sports
squash 39
students, study 131, 134, 156, 159
Sydney Opera House 108, 194

teachers 134–5
Teletubbies 138
television 13–14, 26, 72–3, 138
tennis 48–9
theme songs 14
therapy 77
time wasters 4, 13–18, 21, 66–8, 84–5, 186–7
travel 105–7, 115, 117, 206

Vegemite 144
vegetables 103, 143

Web events 199
Webcams 53, 104–5, 110–11, 113, 117–18
Web-only media 28–9
White Pages 209
wine 101

youth, sites for or by 33, 120, 130–2, 159

zines 26, 32, 33, 62, 150